Lake Tahoe Tourist Guide, USA

Tour North Lake Tahoe, South Lake Tahoe

Author
Caleb Gray.

SONITTEC PUBLISHING. All rights reserved. No part of this publication may be reproduced, distributed, or transmitted in any form or by any means, including photocopying, recording, or other electronic or mechanical methods, without the prior written permission of the publisher, except in the case of brief quotations embodied in critical reviews and certain other noncommercial uses permitted by copyright law. For permission requests, write to the publisher, addressed "Attention: Permissions Coordinator," at the address below.

Copyright © 2019 Sonittec Publishing
All Rights Reserved

First Printed: 2019.

Publisher:
SONITTEC LTD
College House, 2nd Floor
17 King Edwards Road,
Ruislip
London
HA4 7AE

Table of Content

SUMMARY	1
INTRODUCTION	4
HISTORY AND TOURISTIC FACT OF TAHOE	6
NORTH LAKE TAHOE BECOMES A DESTINATION AREA	8
CASINOS AND GAMING	9
WINTER SPORTS SPARK YEAR-ROUND ENTHUSIASM	10
NORTH LAKE TAHOE TODAY	11
LAKE TAHOE TRAVEL GUIDE:	12
My Experience	12
How to Get to Lake Tahoe	29
Lake Tahoe Hiking Trails Guide	33
Lake Tahoe 4th Of July Independent Day	39
Lake Tahoe Ski Guide & Resorts	41
North Lake Tahoe Ski Resorts	42
Lake Tahoe in the Summer	43
LAKE TAHOE RECREATION	52
North Lake Tahoe Recreation	52
Winter Recreation	53
Adventures and Tours	53
Lake Tahoe Ski Packages	54
Discover Lake Tahoe, Inc.	54
Granlibakken Treetop Adventure Park	55
High Sierra Water Ski School	56
Sierra Air Helicopters	57
Squaw Valley Adventure Center	57
Squaw Valley High Camp	58
Tahoe Adventure Company	58
Tahoe Galactic Tours	59
Tributary Whitewater Tours	59
Truckee River Raft Co.	60
Cross Country Skiing	60
Northstar Cross Country Telemark & Snowshoe Center	61
Resort at Squaw Creek Nordic Center	61
Royal Gorge Cross Country Resort	62
Sugar Pine Point State Park	63
Tahoe City Winter Sports Park	66
Tahoe Donner Cross Country Center	67
Tahoe XC, Tahoe City	68
Ice Skating	69
Olympic Ice Pavilion at Squaw Valley Resort	70
Village at Northstar Ice Rink	70

- Ski Resorts..71
  - Alpine Meadows Ski Resort...72
  - Boreal Ski Resort 75
  - Diamond Peak Ski Resort 76
  - Donner Ski Ranch 78
  - Granlibakken Ski Area..79
  - Homewood Ski Resort 80
  - Mt. Rose Ski Resort..81
  - Northstar at Tahoe Ski Resort 83
  - Soda Springs Ski Resort...84
  - Squaw Valley Ski Resort 86
  - Sugar Bowl Ski Resort 88
  - Tahoe Donner Ski Resort...90
- Ski and Snowboard Rentals..91
- Sledding, Tubing and Snowparks 94
  - Boreal's Tubing Park at Playland 95
  - Granlibakken Ski Area..96
  - Northstar Tubing Center 98
- Snowmobiling..99
- Summer Recreation 102
  - North Lake Tahoe Beaches..102
    - Carnelian West Beach...103
    - Chambers Landing...104
    - Chimney Beach...105
    - Commons Beach...106
    - D.L. Bliss State Park, Lester Beach 107
    - Hidden Beach...109
    - Hurricane Bay Beach...111
    - Incline Beach & Private Incline Beaches....................111
    - Kings Beach State Park and Boat Launch 113
    - Meeks Bay Resort and Marina......................................114
    - North Lake Tahoe Beach 115
    - Sand Harbor..116
    - Secret Cove Beach 117
    - Skunk Harbor..119
    - Sugar Pine Point State Park..120
    - Tahoe Vista Recreation Area and Boat Launch........124
  - North Lake Tahoe Bike Rentals..124
    - Cyclepaths Mountain Bike...125
  - North Lake Tahoe Bike Trails..126
    - Brockway Summit to Watson Lake 127
    - Emigrant Trail..128
    - Flume Trail Mountain Bike Trail...................................130
    - Glenshire Lake...131
    - Northstar Mountain Bike Park......................................132

  Sawtooth Trail 132
  Tahoe XC, Tahoe City 134
Boating and Watersports 135
  Action Watersports... 136
  High Sierra Water Ski School 136
  Tahoe City Marina and Mall.. 138
  Tahoe City Marine Supply.. 139
  Tahoe Eco-Sports 140
  Tahoe Paddle & Oar 140
  Tahoe Water Adventures 140
  Truckee River Rafting 141
Camping and RV Parks.. 143
  D.L. Bliss State Park, Lester Beach... 143
  General Creek Campground at Sugar Pine State Park 145
  Kaspian Campground 146
  Lake Forest Campground... 147
  Meeks Bay Campground 147
  Mt. Rose Campground 148
Fishing and Charters.. 149
  Captain Chris Fishing Charters 150
  Chuck's Bait, Tackle & Guide Service.. 150
  Kingfish Guide Service 151
  Mickey's Big Mack Charters... 151
  Sierra Fin Addicts Guide Service... 152
  Thy Rod & Staff 152
Golf Courses 153
  Tahoe Donner Golf Course 154
  Coyote Moon Golf Course 154
  Incline Village Championship Golf Course 155
  Incline Village Mountain Golf Course 156
  Northstar at Tahoe Golf Course 157
  Old Brockway Golf Course 158
  Old Greenwood Golf Course... 159
  Ponderosa Golf Course.. 160
  Resort at Squaw Creek Golf Course... 161
  Tahoe City Golf Course.. 161
Tahoe Hiking.. 162
  Brockway Summit to Watson Lake.. 163
  Desolation Wilderness 164
  Emigrant Trail 166
  Glenshire Lake 167
  Prey Meadows / Skunk Harbor 168
  Sawtooth Trail 169
  Tahoe XC, Tahoe City 170
Horseback Riding 171

        Alpine Meadows Stable 171
        Tahoe Donner Equestrian Center 172
        Verdi Trails West Ranch 173
    North Lake Tahoe Marinas... 173
        Kings Beach State Park and Boat Launch 173
        Meeks Bay Marina.. 175
        Obexers Marina.. 175
        Sand Harbor Boat Ramp.. 176
        Tahoe City Marina and Mall 177
        Tahoe Vista Recreation Area and Boat Launch......................... 178

OUTDOOR SPORTS 178
    Hiking in South Lake Tahoe 178
        Advanced Hiking in South Lake Tahoe 180
    Winter Sports 181
    Downhill at Heavenly 184
    Summer Activities... 186
    Biking South Lake Tahoe 188
    Mountain Biking South Lake Tahoe 189
    The Truckee River 191
    Lake Tahoe Snowshoeing.. 193
    Crusing Lake Tahoe.. 194
    Lake Tahoe Wakeboarding.. 196
    Lake Tahoe Parks.. 198
    Stateline, Nv.. 199
    Emerald Bay 202
    North Lake Tahoe 203
    Interesting Small Nevada Towns 205
    Tahoe's Western Shore.. 207
    Lakes of South Lake Tahoe 209

OTHER THINGS TO DO IN SOUTH LAKE TAHOE 210
    Why South Lake Tahoe?... 212
    Heavenly Village Shopping 214
    Shopping in South Lake Tahoe 216
    Shopping in South Lake Tahoe 217
    South Lake Tahoe Eateries 219
    Lake Tahoe Antiques.. 221
    Lake Tahoe Weddings.. 223
    Relaxation at The Beach Club.. 224

Summary

The importance of travelling in our life?

Everyone has their very own reasons to travel. Some people travel for work, some travel for pleasure while for others it is just a way of life. They travel to live and to escape at the same time.

Whatever might be the reason to travel, here are few ways in which travelling would definitely change you and I think that is why travelling becomes so important in life:

Enjoy being alone: There is something therapeutic about being alone and being at peace with it. While you soak in a new culture, you also connect with your own inner self.

Learn to adapt: It is a different world out there, literally. Be it the pace of life, the language or simply the change in weather, it is always a change and you have to adapt to it. This is what makes travelling truly beautiful as you break away from the routine and adapt to something totally new.

Experience a new culture: Every place comes with its distinct cultural habits, you cannot think about New York without talking about its fast paced life and about Italy without enjoying its relaxed lifestyle. Similarly, while visiting the UK you might have to be a bit formal in your interactions with the locals, on the other hand, while greeting the people in Thailand, one can be really warm and casual.

Broaden your taste buds: Travelling without experiencing the local food is just not complete. It is not only a culinary experience but a cultural one as well.

Get out of comfort zone: From simple experiences like the weather, way of life or food to the more adventurous ones like trying a new sport, travelling really pushes ones boundaries to the core. You might end up participating in a street carnival in Brazil just like the locals or trying the local delicacies (read insects) in Thailand.

Indulge in Photography: It does not matter whether you are a professional or not. It is also irrelevant whether you have a DSLR or a very basic camera, while travelling what matters is the love and quest for seeing beautiful places and the sheer joy of capturing them in your lense. Travelling would in return give you your very own collection of amazing postcards of beautiful sunsets, snow laced mountains or sunny beaches.

Learn to escape: Travelling is the best way to break the routine. If you are in a bustling city, go ahead and experience the country life. If you are in a rural place, travel to a bustling city and experience its madness. Stressed with the city life or work pressure? A spa break in Himalayas or Kerala is a must try.

Appreciate Nature: The quest to explore more when one is travelling always leads to a sense of amazement about nature. While most of us keep a track of technological advancements, Nature has its own ways of outshining all of these. The Antelope Canyon in Arizona or Turquoise Ice in Russia are the finest examples of this. For more, check out the most unbelievable places around the world.

Get closer to your own roots: While one travels and experiences a lot of different cultures and practices, it definitely brings one closer to his or her own roots. Travel helps one appreciate one's identity and culture.

Travelling is all about experiences. They can happen in terms of culture, people, places but most importantly with one's own self and this was all about

Introduction

Whether you swim, fish, sail, or simply rest on its shores, you'll be wowed by the overwhelming beauty of Lake Tahoe, the largest alpine lake in North America. Famous for its cobalt-blue water and surrounding snowcapped peaks, Lake Tahoe straddles the state line between California and Nevada. The border gives this popular Sierra Nevada resort region a split personality. About half its visitors are intent on low-key sightseeing, hiking, camping, and boating. The rest head directly to the Nevada side, where bargain dining, big-name entertainment, and the lure of a jackpot draw them into the glittering casinos.

To explore the lake area and get a feel for its many differing communities, drive the 72-mile road that follows the shore through wooded flatlands and past beaches, climbing to vistas on the rugged southwest side of the lake and passing through busy commercial developments and casinos on its northeastern and southeastern edges. Another option is to actually go out *on* the 22-mile-long, 12-mile-wide lake on a sightseeing cruise or kayaking trip.

The lake, the communities around it, the state parks, national forests, and protected tracts of wilderness are the region's main draws, but other nearby destinations are gaining in popularity. Truckee, with an Old West feel and innovative restaurants, entices visitors looking for a relaxed pace and easy access to Tahoe's north shore and Olympic Valley ski parks. And today Reno, once known only for its casinos, attracts tourists with its buzzing arts scene, downtown riverfront, and campus events at the University of Nevada.

History and Touristic Fact of Tahoe

Tahoe history tells how the Sierra persisted as major obstacle for pioneers trying to reach the California land of milk and honey with dreams of gold mining. But there was no holding back and the westward migration was steady.

In 1849, with the advent of the California Gold Rush, the emigrant influx morphed into a flood, and passes to the north and south of the Basin sustained considerable pioneer traffic. The first East-West road to carve directly across the mountains was the "Bonanza Road," built after the 1859 discovery of the Comstock Lode in Virginia City. Today, this route is known as Highway 50.

The Comstock Lode, which emerged as the richest known deposit of silver in the U.S., turned Virginia City into a metropolis of 20,000, gaining Nevada statehood and developing the area into a center of wealth and culture. The effect on Tahoe was not quite as positive. Between 1860 and 1890, nearly all of the trees in the Tahoe Basin were logged to provide wood for the complex underground tunnels and excavation. The demise of the Comstock Lode just before the turn of the century could not have occurred soon enough; evidence of this extensive logging can still be seen today in the area's forests.

During the 1850s, San Francisco's population had grown significantly to where the city's inhabitants required communication with the rest of the world. The snowy winters and high climbs of the Sierra Nevada, made carrying the mail a dangerous job. After two brave souls failed to regularly complete the route via mule pack. This changed when Norwegian-born John "Snowshoe" Thompson, now part of Tahoe history, used the snowshoes his father had rigged for him in combination with a rudimentary pair of skis to make the 90-mile trek up and over the Sierra to the Carson Valley. Twice monthly, carrying a pack weighing more than 100 pounds, Thompson completed the eastern-bound route in only 3 days.

The western section of the transcontinental railroad was completed in 1868, extending the Central Pacific Railroad via Donner Pass at Donner Lake. The line, which still functions today, winds roughly along the Truckee River, clinging to granite walls, crossing bridges, and passing through tunnels that protect the train from the winter snows. Much of this portion of the railway can be seen from Highway 80 and is an impressive feat of engineering. The current tunnels are a ridgeline to the south from the Snowshed tube. But, you can explore the abandoned eerie lengths of the original "Snowshed Tunnels" that snake along the mountains over Donner Lake.

The first automobile arrived in Tahoe in 1905 in the form of a chain-driven Simplex. The car's not-so-humble owner, Mrs. Joseph Chanslor, completed the trip from Sacramento in only eight hours. In 1913, the Lincoln Highway crossed the Sierra as part of the first coast-to-coast paved route. Though replaced by US 40 in 1930, sections of this road are open during the summer as scenic, historic drives.

The introduction of these fast, load-bearing transcontinental routes immediately increased the flow of raw goods, manufactured products and people in and out of California. Railway and roadside stops throughout the Sierra exposed more travelers to the beauty of the Tahoe Basin and created a buzz about the area as a viable vacation destination.

North Lake Tahoe Becomes a Destination Area

By the late 19th century, Lake Tahoe had become a popular vacation spot for wealthy San Francisco residents. Beginning in 1887, Robert M. Watson, who later became Tahoe's first constable, ran an inn called the Tahoe House with his wife and five children. In 1901, the original Tahoe Tavern was constructed by Walter Danforth Bliss. Over the next several decades, the Tavern was expanded to include such amenities as a casino with a bowling alley, ballroom (which was later converted to a movie theater), physician's office, laundry, steam plant and water system. Both the Tahoe House and Tahoe Tavern were located in Tahoe City on the West Shore. Today, modern buildings bearing the same names commemorate their existence. Other notable hotels and residencies around the Lake included the Glenbrook Inn on the East Shore; Tallac House on the West Shore; and Brockway Springs Hotel near Crystal Bay, which was originally constructed as a getaway for Comstock miners.

In 1904, when Tahoe House owner Watson returned from trying his luck at gold mining, North Lake Tahoe was so well populated that the citizens decided a full-time constable was necessary, and they elected Watson to the position. Watson, who was known to local youth as "Grandpa," is famous for having declared the Tahoe City jail unsuitable even for miscreants and allowing prisoners to sleep on his kitchen floor.

Guests of these popular resorts could take a South Pacific train from San Francisco all the way to Truckee. The Lake Tahoe Railway would then take them into Tahoe City, where they either settled down into one of the nearby lodging options, or climbed aboard a steamship that could deliver them to several spots around the Lake.

Casinos and Gaming

For many early visitors Tahoe's prime attractions were the casinos that opened up on the North Shore after the turn of the 19thcentury. In 1927 the Ta-Neva-Ho (present-day Cal-Neva Resort) opened as the first casino in Crystal Bay. The Tahoe Biltmore, among others, soon followed. The Cal-Neva was built by Bob Sherman and in subsequent years saw a series of short-lived and occasionally famous owners, including Frank Sinatra. Sinatra's contributions to the resort included the Celebrity Showroom and a helicopter pad on the roof to aid transportation for some of his wealthier guests. Frequent patrons at that time included Marilynn Monroe, Dean Martin, Sammy Davis, Jr., and mobster Sam Giancana. The mobsters ended Ol' Blue Eyes' casino gaming ventures. For more about the history of the Cal-Neva Resort Spa and Casino...

Winter Sports Spark Year-Round Enthusiasm

Modern recreational skiing in the Sierra dates back to 1938, when the bravest Bay Area souls found their ways up to present-day Sugar Bowl mountain peaks via the Southern Pacific Railroad. Walt Disney, Austrian Hannes Schroll and a few others had the foresight to recognize the area's potential as a world-class ski resort, and in 1938 Sugar Bowl officially opened. The resort would go on to build the first ski lift in California, and to this day is a second home to some of the Bay Area's most established families.

Meanwhile, the Lake Tahoe Ski Club had already put the North Shore on the map for winter recreation, having hosted the 1931 and 1932 Winter Olympic Tryouts. National Jumping and Cross-Country competitions all took place at present-day Granlibakken, then known as Olympic Hill and owned by the Tahoe Tavern.

In 1960, Tahoe's reputation for winter sports gained international recognition when Squaw Valley hosted the Winter Olympics. North Lake Tahoe tourism benefited greatly from the exposure, as these were the first Olympic Games to be televised. Many of the resorts, motels, restaurants and ski lifts built to accommodate the influx of Olympians and fans still proudly host guests today.

North Lake Tahoe Today

With a total population of 65,000 and approximately 3 million visitors each year, the Tahoe Basin remains the same awe-inspiring place that drew the Washoe Indians here 10 thousand years ago. Tourism booms as the area's main source of income, while visitors and locals alike bask in the outdoor and indoor recreational options available at every turn. North Lake Tahoe continues to produce nationally ranked athletes year after year; the rich and famous continue to flock here; and the wildlife continues to abound. Most importantly though, the Lake remains an icon of American history, tradition and values.

Lake Tahoe Travel Guide:

My Experience

Discover The Best That Lake Tahoe Has to Offer
"To breathe the same air as angels, you must go to Tahoe." -- Mark Twain

I sat with angst as I awaited to deplane. I had just landed at Reno International Airport. Next stop? Lake Tahoe. A place I hadn't visited since I was 3 years old. "Do you remember it at all?" my mother asked at some point before the trip. "Kind of," I replied. But in all sincerity, the memories were hazy. Like the fog that drifts into a valley, idly obscuring and clouding your vision, I couldn't really recall it.

I remembered snow. Yes. That was it. Blankets and blankets of snow. Sheets stretching as far as the eye could see. I remembered the sounds of laughter. Carving snow angels. Building snowmen. People skiing. Falling and collapsing. Shaking off the fresh powder. Getting back up. But my hazy memories of fun in the snow were just one part of the Lake Tahoe experience. Yes. I visited North Lake Tahoe's peaks. But that was some 30 odd years before.

So I thought about it for a moment. I reflected on the enormity of the task ahead. I knew I had my work cut out for me. I knew I had to describe a destination that was home to approximately 30,000 year-round residents. But also a destination that attracts roughly 3 million people per year. How was I going to take it all in? In 3 days, no less. That, I wasn't sure of. I just knew that in order to create a luxury travel guide about Lake Tahoe, I just had to go there.

The funny thing? I had read and consumed a wealth of blog posts about the Tahoe experience. I had watched dozens of videos on YouTube attempting to educate people about traveling here. From things you should see to what you should do. But still, it didn't provide me with a sense of the true iconic beauty that awaited me. The truth? You can't simply call Lake Tahoe beautiful. Especially without ever seeing it in person.

Sure, it's a beautiful place. But it's also so much more than that. It's an earthly haven. An iconic lake that straddles both California and Nevada. A travel destination like none other. I'd go so far as describing it as Utopian. Yes. Utopian is the right word. Because, when you're here, you feel it. It's like you've just arrived at a place so breathtaking, the words evade you.

As if the scent of pine and crisp mountain air is so intoxicating, that it leaves you bewildered. How can I describe Lake Tahoe to you? How can I possibly get across this surreal experience of being here? Sure, I can try. That is, by chance, why you're reading this travel guide. You want to know what's in store for you in Tahoe. Right? Fair enough. All you need to do is imagine what heaven on earth would be like. And there you have it.

No. I'm dead serious. Heaven on earth quite possibly comes just about as close as it gets to an accurate depiction of Lake Tahoe. It's awe-inspiring. Truly. It's the type of beauty that takes your breath away. Snow-capped mountains in the distance. Shimmering lake waters that spill out for miles in every direction. The untouched beauty of Mother Nature. Pine and Fir trees that wind and twist their way into the heavens.

From the golden-sanded shores of Sand Harbor to the snow-covered peaks of Northstar and others, Tahoe has it all. From luxurious lakefront cabins on its south shore, to the epic cabins that dot the hillsides of the North. From the exhilarating thrill of casinos on the Nevada state line to the picturesque beauty of small villages that dot the lake's circumference, it's all here. And it's waiting for you. Right now.

But knowing I had to create a luxury travel guide for Tahoe definitely put the pressure on. As I walked off that plane, I wondered how I was going to soak it all in. With a 72-mile circumference, and loads of beaches and peaks, how was I going to see enough of Lake Tahoe to truly be able to create a comprehensive guide? That's all I could think about as I walked off that plane. It was game time.

The North Shore of Lake Tahoe wasn't my first stop. It was Truckee. It seeps small-town charm. A place where smiles and hello's and how-are-you's were genuinely asked. You can't beat these places. You just can't. Especially when you're so used to big-city life. But this place is genuine. Downtown Historic Truckee, they call it. A small strip of quaint shops line a main drag here.

This town has been reborn. From a once-upon-a-time logging village to an upscale ski destination, things have definitely changed for Historic Truckee. And walking the great stroll amidst the shops and bakeries and ice cream parlors that line its main street in Downtown Historic Truckee, you certainly feel it. With roughly 16,000 inhabitants, this cozy spot is just an earshot from the lake.

In the distance, mountains lined with Fir and Pine trees blanket the horizon. In 1900, the Southern Pacific Railroad built a wood depot here that served as a transit hub. Trains would go in and out, arriving empty and departing full of Cedars and Redwoods and Pines. In the distance, you can still hear the trains roar by. Today, it's an Amtrak train that chugs along.

In the mornings, the train bound for the west arrives from Chicago and Denver. It's heading towards Sacramento. The eastbound train arrives in the mid-afternoon, heading for Eastern seaboard. The trains are iconic. They're part of American history. And they're what make this quaint town so special.

But as I strolled that main drag, I wasn't thinking about trains. I wasn't thinking about shopping either. What was on my mind? Food. All I could think about was food. I was famished to say the least. So hungry that I had to dip into a pizzeria before my group arrived. I wasn't expecting anything amazing.

The place I chose? Best Pies. A pizzeria. Growing up in New York, I was used to go good pizzas. We call them "pies" in the East, so I knew what was in store for me. Flashbacks of heavenly gooey cheese-filled thin-crusts danced in my mind. The best part? I wasn't disappointed.

The service was impeccable. A friendly smile. Great food. Good conversation.. I just ducked in. From there, it was off to Marty's Cafe to meet my group. Another great place to eat. In fact, Truckee is filled with these little spots. Where they take food seriously. Like mama's home cooking.

When you're heading to Tahoe, stop off in Truckee. Take the time to stroll around this town. Look around. Patronize the shops. Eat in the restaurants. This is small town living. If you're from a big city, it'll come as a shock to the system. But a pleasant one. You'll be over-the-moon happy that you visited this quaint little spot.

The best part? There are plenty of things to do nearby. In fact, if you're heading to Tahoe in the winter, this small town is ideally located between a variety of peaks and museums and even river rafting. From Donner Memorial State Park to the Northstar California resort, and plenty in between, you'll find so many *things to do here near Truckee*.

Donner Memorial State Park

Just east of where the I-80 and Highway-89 meet, just a hop, skip and a jump from Historic Downtown Truckee, is Donner Memorial State Park. Although I didn't get a chance to personally check it out, the site offers three miles of lake frontage at Donner Lake along with easy access to Donner Creek.

If you're into fishing, camping or hiking, this is the place to be. In the summer, it's a mecca for outdoor activities. Hills of granite and towering Pine trees cluster in groups amidst the mountainous landscape. Wildlife roams free. Birds call from above. Squirrels scurry across in search of food. And the scant Black Bear or Coyote is known to roam these parts. So be wary.

In the winter, you can cross-country ski or snowshoe across trails that lead you around beautiful ridges that rise violently from the earth's crust. You can visit the park year-round. But, keep in mind, to fish, you'll need a license and to camp, you'll need to make a reservation on the ReserveCalifornia.com website or call 1-800-444-7275 for more details.

In the park, you'll discover a pioneer statue. It was fashioned in respect to the emigrants who made their voyage through the Sierra Nevada

Northstar California

Set amidst one of the most serene environments on earth, Northstar California is one of the most epic ski destinations on earth. It boasts 19 separate ski lifts. An 18-hole golf course. A cross-country ski center. And a stunning central village along with high-end accommodations. Whether you're heading to *North Lake Tahoe in the winter*, or the summer, it's an idyllic, serene spot.

In fact, Northstar was my ultimate destination in Lake Tahoe. It's where we stayed in a luxurious townhome. *Stella Nova Northstar*, to be precise. Situated directly on the slopes, the property was a true ski-in and ski-out. If you're looking for a North Lake Tahoe cabin, I would highly suggest that one.

Northstar is a high-end resort destination located just 200 miles (322 kilometers) from the San Francisco Bay Area. It's owned by EPR Properties. Purchased in 2016 from CNL Lifestyle Properties for $456 million. It's an epic destination.

The amenities here are outstanding. They call the common house "The Tree House" and it's a place where you can relax, unwind and even have your own expert concierge they call "Outfitters."

Outfitters know the ins-and-outs of Lake Tahoe. They'll tell you where to hike. Where to bike. Where to ski. Where to paddleboard. And, generally, where to do just about anything in the area. To top it off, The Tree House is filled with its own amenities.

Downstairs, a personal fitness center. Outside, a heated swimming pool. You'll also discover a hot tub. Steam room. Pool table. Tabletop shuffleboard. Leather couches. High-end flat-screen televisions. Sonos-powered sound systems. Fridges filled with wines and beers and bottled waters. Snacks such as protein bars. An espresso machine. And so much more.

Historic Downtown Truckee
Historic Downtown Truckee is a must-see in North Lake Tahoe. It's filled with quaint shops and bakeries and restaurants. They reside in historic brick buildings that are steeped in the town's rich past. With just 16,000 inhabitants, it's certainly got that small town charm. Once a logging village, it's now been transformed into a high-end ski destination.

Originally named, Coburn Station, it was renamed to Truckee in honor of a Paiute Chief, Trukizo. It was his tribe that the first European settlers encountered when they came across the perilous Sierra Nevada mountain range.

If you're a fan of Charlie Chaplin, his comedy, The Gold Rush, which premiered in 1925, was shot in Truckee during its first two weeks of production. It was also the setting for the true book, Citizen Jane, which debuted in 1999. It's also the town featured in the video game, American Truck Simulator.

The town is filled with historic sites that you just can't miss. The Truckee Hotel, which was built way back in 1873, was originally named the American House. The name was later changed to the Whitney House until 1976 when it was renamed the Truckee Hotel. In 1992, it received an extensive renovation that restored the entire building, its exterior and interior space.

In Downtown Historic Truckee, you can still visit the Old Jail. It was originally built in 1875 and it was used to house inmates for over 90 years until 1964. Today, visitors can tour through the Old Jail Museum. Open to the public, it's one of very few surviving 19th Century jails that are still standing today.

Boreal Mountain Resort
Situated just west of Truckee, off Highway 80, in Soda Springs, Boreal Mountain Resort is a Lake Tahoe fixture, and typically one of the first resorts to open in the year for skiing and snowboarding.

The resort has nine chair lifts, and compared to some of the other mountain resorts, it's relatively tiny.

The base of Boreal Mountain Resort is located at 7,200 feet (2,194 meters). It has a summit that reaches 10,067 feet (3,068 meters), one of the tallest peaks in Lake Tahoe. The longest run you'll find here is approximately 1 mile (about 1.6 km) and the biggest vertical drop on the mountain is around 500 feet (152 meters).

The resort also has an epic Terrain Park. It's perfect for snowboarders. You'll find boxes and handrails and super-half-pipes here. There's also a family snow play area, for those who are a little less experienced.

Whitewater Rafting

Whitewater rafting on the Truckee River is usually done at one of the most common spots on the river called the River Ranch Run. This stars from around where Lake Tahoe outlets into the Truckee River and it extends all the way down for about 3 miles (4.8 km) to River Ranch Restaurant.

This run is all class 1 and class 2. Class 1 rafting includes small rough areas and will require some maneuvering with a very basic skill level required. Class 2 rafting includes some rough waters along with rocks and it will usually require some basic paddling skills. Overall, this run is primarily for beginners.

Tahoe Donner Downhill Ski

The Tahoe Donner Downhill Ski Resort is part of the Tahoe Donner community. Over 7,200 pristine acres of blissful mountainside along with approximately 6,500 properties. It's situated approximately 25 minutes from Lake Tahoe, in Truckee. Tahoe Donner Downhill Ski Resort has been around for 50 years.

The resort offers one quad-chair lift, 1 double-chair lift, and 3 conveyor lifts. The terrain is made up of approximately 40% novice slopes and 60% intermediate. You'll find 17 total runs here, 3 terrain parks and around 120 skiable acres.

Truckee Railroad Museum
Truckee is a town steeped in history. As an old logging and railroad locale, it's fitting to have a museum dedicated to the history of the area's railroads. In fact, the entrance to the museum is an old caboose from Southern Pacific Railroad. It was used in the area. And the color scheme matches the old paint scheme for Southern Pacific.

Railroads have played a major role in Truckee's development. In fact, the first transcontinental railroad, which connected the east to the west, completing the link across America, had an important train yard in Truckee. That railroad was completed on May 10th, 1869. But it was a feat of sheer brute force and will.

It took two years for workers to bore a hole through the Donner Summit. That tunnel is 1,659 feet long (505 meters). While it was being completed, workers were still laying track and hauling materials to complete the Truckee River Canyon route. Railroads played such a huge role in Truckee's history that it only makes sense that an entire museum was dedicated to it.

This is the ideal stop to take your children. Or, if you're simply interested in railroads or in the rich history of Truckee and trains through the Sierra Nevada, this is a must-see during your stop in the Lake Tahoe area. The museum is located at 10075 Donner Pass Road in Truckee

Old Truckee Jail Museum

The Old Jail is Downtown Historic Truckee's original jail that was built in 1875. It's still standing. It was used to house inmates through 1964. And originally built in 1875. For 90 years it served to house inmates. Today, you can tour through the Old Jail Museum since it's open to the general public. To this day, it's one of the only few surviving 19th Century jails in existence in the United States.

Soda Springs Mountain Ski Resort

Soda Springs is an area in Truckee situated 3 miles (4.8 km) west of Donner Pass. The Soda Springs Mountain Ski Resort is the longest-running ski resort in the state of California. This is one of the best places to explore the epic winters of Lake Tahoe. Granite cliffs and

Pine-tree covered mountainsides make this a picturesque and scenic destination in Tahoe for all things winter-sport related.

The base at Soda Springs is situated at 6,700 feet (2,042 meters), while its summit is at 7,352 feet (2,240 meters). The longest ski run you'll find here is just 0.4 miles (0.64km) and the biggest vertical drop is 652 feet (198 meters). That pales in comparison to some of the other ski resorts in Lake Tahoe. But if you're not an intermediate or advanced skier, Soda Springs Mountain Ski Resort is a great place to start your education

Golfing at Old Greenwood Golf Course

In the spring and summer months, Lake Tahoe is a haven for golf. Near Truckee, you'll find several courses. Golfing at Old Greenwood Golf Course is one of those courses. The course is nestled in Old Greenwood, an upscale resort community. Here, you'll discover sprawling custom-built cabins and homes nestled deep within 600 acres of pristine towering-Pine-and-Fir covered landscape.

Old Greenwood is a Jack Nicklaus Signature Golf Course. Designed with the meticulous detail of a master golfer, no expense was spared in creating Old Greenwood. But the grand design was more about sculpting the course and blending it with Mother Nature. Not about grandeur. Here, you'll also discover the Tahoe Mountain Club.

At Old Greenwood, you'll actually discover two distinct golf courses. Old Greenwood Golf Course is one of them. Gray's Crossing Golf Course is the other. Both are 18 holes of sheer perfection. However, while Old Greenwood was designed by Jack Nicklaus, Gray's Crossing was the brainchild of Peter Jacobsen.

The Best Cabins in Lake Tahoe

I don't know about you, but I'm a fan of opulent luxury. I'm talking about crystal chandeliers and distressed hardwoods and marble finishes. I'm talking about accommodations that take your breath away. Not just homes. Mansions. Glorified cabins you can rent year round no matter what the occasion. The best part? Lake Tahoe is littered with luxury cabins and resorts that you can call home.

My trip to Tahoe was purposeful. I wanted to see what living large in Tahoe really meant. I was looking for mountain luxury. Cabins that were able to masterfully blend mountain living with refined elegance. Truthfully? There's no such thing as "too luxurious" in my mind. Now, I'm not talking about the Ritz Carlton, which you can definitely find in Lake Tahoe.

To me, the ideal luxury cabin in Lake Tahoe should be held to a certain standard. And, surprisingly, I had my fill of touring some of the most luxurious homes that Tahoe has to offer. And to put it briefly. I was awe-inspired by some of the homes. There's a truly refined taste and luxurious standard of living here. It doesn't exist everywhere. But for those who enjoy the good life, you can certainly find it here.

North Lake Vs South Lake

Before going any further, there's one distinction we need to make. There's quite a difference between North Lake Tahoe and South Lake Tahoe. It's a different vibe. Different energy. You can feel it. Now, depending on your speed, you might prefer one over the other. For me? It's the north all the way. I just can't describe it. But being in North Lake Tahoe was spectacular.

It wasn't just the cabins in the north. It was everything. Yes, it's closer to the airport than the south. But it's so much more than that. Now, it's also important to note that the North has way more peaks than the south does. However, some of the peaks you'll find in the south are truly outrageous. For example, Heavenly Mountain Resort boasts the longest ski run (5.5 miles) and biggest vertical drop (3502 feet). That's pretty spectacular if you're into outrageously daring snowsports.

However, all else being equal, I'd choose the North any day of the year over the south. But that doesn't mean you won't love the south. For example, we toured the Sierra Shores Lakefront Townhomes in South Lake Tahoe and they were awe-inspiring. Directly on the lakefront, it's a site to marvel at. And the interiors of the townhomes were nothing short of luxurious.

Overall, you'll want to choose the south if you're heading in during the summer months. South Lake Tahoe also seems to be where the party's at. But if you're looking for real opulence, it's the north all the way. I'd also much prefer the north in the winter months. You have 10 peaks to choose from in the north as opposed to 4 in the south. But, keep in mind that the north is also going to run you a pretty penny.

Both the cabins in North Lake Tahoe and the South Lake Tahoe rentals are pricey. Don't get me wrong. But the north outstrips the south. There's far more opulence here. Elegance. Extravagance. Cabins where wind and glass and stone unite in an explosive array of fine mountain living. Marbles and granites and cedars and pines all reflect the outdoor elements of the outdoor environment.

So which one do you choose? The north or the south? It's simply a matter of taste. I polled people on this very question on a Facebook page called I Love Lake Tahoe and the replies varied. But, the north won out over the south by about 3 to 2. Now, that's not a huge difference. Again, it's a personal preference. Some simply love the south for the summers and others adore the north for the winters. Where you stay depends entirely on you.

North Lake Tahoe Cabins

With 10 peaks to choose from in the north, there's plenty to do here. That's especially true in the winter. But where you're looking to stay for a few days or even a few weeks at a time, there are plenty of incredible cabins in North Lake Tahoe to choose from. InvitedHome features a portfolio of hand-picked homes in North Lake that represent the best of the best.

Whether you're into the truly elegant and opulent, or you're in the mood for rustic luxury, you'll discover it here in North Lake. This is a truly serene and picturesque setting. A place where vistas and views abound. Where snow-capped mountains tower in the distance. Where the lake shimmers and sparkles in full glory from your perch high up in the hills.

North Lake is truly inspiring. Not just from a sense of elegance. But also the serenity of this area. You can feel it. You can breathe it in the air. It's infectious. The people and scenery and the awe-inspiring views from the many vantage points on the hillsides. This is where magical memories are made

South Lake Tahoe Cabins

If you're heading to Lake Tahoe for some good old-fashioned summer fun, then South Lake Tahoe is the place to be. It's one of the most sought-after summer destinations in the United States, and there's prime access to a large swath of the lake from here.

South Lake Tahoe is where you'll discover casinos and luxurious lakefront townhomes. It's where you'll find Stateline and nightlife. Bars and pub crawls and discos. Much less reserved than its northern counterpart, South Lake Tahoe is the place to be if you're looking to let go and just have an uninhibited great time.

When it comes to accommodation, there's no shortage of vacation rentals in South Lake. In fact, you'll find the area teeming with cabins. From lakefront communities like Sierra Shores to more upscale standalone cabins, you can find a wide range here in South Lake of short-term rentals to choose from.

How to Get to Lake Tahoe

If you're heading to Tahoe, you're likely heading to Reno International Airport (RNO). That's where I landed at least. That's also where 3.5 million other folks land each and every year. A lion's share of them heading to Tahoe. And it's ideally situated for that. Located just 35 miles northeast of the northern shores of the lake, you can reach it in about 30 to 40 minutes depending on traffic.

If you're heading to the South Shore, you're looking at roughly an hour to an hour-and-a-half or more from the airport. Again, it all depends on traffic. The cool part? Tahoe is deeply embedded in the Sierra Nevada mountains. As you drive from that airport and make your way towards the lake, you ascend and descend across those mountains.

The view as you reach the top is spectacular. Yes, even from the highway.

It's as if you've been transported to another dimension. A place where one heavenly view trumps another one. Each time you gaze out, you wonder if you've ever seen something so spellbinding before in your life - and you haven't even started any of the *activities that await you in Tahoe*. In those 40 or so minutes it takes you to reach the north shores of the lake, you'll gasp and gaze with eyes wide open. You will. I'm sure of it.

Before you ever travel to Lake Tahoe, you'll probably ask yourself whether you need to rent a car. The answer? A resounding yes. Lake Tahoe, although not huge by any measure, still is a pretty vast area. Most of the streets twist and wind while dropping and increasing in elevation dramatically in areas. Simply put, not everything is nearby.

While you can rent a taxi in Lake Tahoe or even grab an Uber or Lyft, in the peak and busiest seasons, you'll have a problem getting timely transportation. For that reason, you absolutely should rent a car. Whether you're flying into the Reno International Airport or Sacramento, you can find car rentals from all the popular car rental companies.

In Reno, you'll find 9 rental car agencies, all located in the baggage claim of the airport.

Alamo Car Rental
2001 E Plumb Ln
Reno, NV 89502 US.
Phone : (775)323-7940

Avis Car Rental
Reno-Tahoe Intl Airport (RNO)
Address: 2001 East Plumb Lane, Reno, NV, 89502, U S A
Phone: (1) 775-785-2727
Hours of Operation: Sun - Sat 5:00 AM - 1:00 AM

Dollar Car Rental
RENO, NV
2001 East Plumb Lane
Reno, NV 89502
866-434-2226

Enterprise Car Rental
2001 E Plumb Ln C/o Reno Arpt
Reno, NV, US, 89502
+1 775-325-3977

Hertz Car Rental
Reno Tahoe International Airport
2001 East Plumb Lane
Reno , Nevada 89502
United States
Show me other nearby Hertz Car Rental locations on a map.
Your phone numbers: (775) 785-2554
Your fax number: (775) 323-3061
Location Type: Corporate
Hours of Operation: Mon-Sun 6:00AM-1:00AM

National Car Rental
Reno-Tahoe International Airport (RNO)
2001 E Plumb Ln,
Reno, NV 89502, US
+1 775-323-7940

Thrifty Car Rental
RENO - TAHOE INTERNATIONAL AIRPORT
2001 E Plumb Lane
Reno, NV 89502
(877) 283-0898

Payless Car Rental (actual rental cars are located off-site. Contact the below address and get any other location addreses)
Alabama
Birmingham Intl Airport, AL (BHM)
5900 Messer Airport Hwy
AL, 35212
U S A
 (1) 205-591-7020

Budget Car Rental
Reno-Tahoe Intl Airport (RNO)
Address: Address1 Testing For Rno Budget, Address2 Testing For Rno Budget, Reno, NV, 89502, United States
Phone: (1) 775-785-2409
Hours of Operation: Sun - Sat 5:00 AM - 1:00 AM

If you're dead set against having a car in Lake Tahoe, then you could opt for one of the hotel shuttles that could take you from the airport to your hotel. Of course, if you've rented a condo or cabin in Lake Tahoe, that might not be a possibility. Still, you could opt to grab a taxi from the airport or even take an Uber or a Lyft as well.

However, there are some paid shuttles at the Reno Airport as well. You can find more information about the shuttle service near the baggage claim. You'll find this in the A and B doors. It's just west of the baggage claim. The following three are the paid shuttles you can find in the Reno International Airport:

Airport Mini-Bus Service: 775-786-3700 - www.bell-limo.com

North Lake Tahoe Express: 866-216-5222 - www.northlaketahoeexpress.com

South Tahoe Airporter: 866-898-2463 - www.amadorstagelines.com/lake-tahoe

The complimentary shuttles to their respective hotels are free. You'll find them along the curb outside the D doors of baggage claim.

Atlantis Hotel - This shuttle runs from 4:45 am to 12:15 am at 15 minutes to and past the hour, every hour.

Circus Circus Hotel - This shuttle runs from 4:45 am to 11:45 pm at 15 minutes to and past the hour, every hour.

Grand Sierra Resort & Casino - This shuttle runs from 4:45 am to 12:15 am and departs every 15 minutes from the airport.

Harrah's Reno Resort & Casino - This shuttle runs from 5:00 am to 12:00 am and departs every hour on the hour.

Nugget's Casino Resort - This shuttle runs from 5:30 am to 11:30 pm and departs from the airport every hour at half-past the hour.

Peppermill Hotel - This shuttle runs from 4:45 am to 11:45 pm at 15 minutes to and past the hour, every hour.

Sands Regency - You'll need to call this hotel for airport pickup. You can reach them at 775-348-2200

Silver Legacy - This shuttle runs from 4:45 am to 11:45 pm at 15 minutes to and past the hour, every hour.

If you need more information on how to get to Lake Tahoe, the best transportation from Reno, or where to stay around the lake, get in touch with our Vacation Consultants today. InvitedHome guests receive unparalleled care and attention, and we'll be in touch from booking to checkout to take care of anything you need.

Lake Tahoe Hiking Trails Guide

Lake Tahoe is a haven for hikers. Glacier-carved granite cliffs protrude from mountainsides blanketed with towering Pine and Fir and Spruce trees that spiral towards the heavens. Alpine meadows engulfed in wildflowers in the spring and summer paint the perfect portrait of Mother Nature's sheer beauty.

Whether you're an avid hiker or a novice, you'll discover a hiking trail in Lake Tahoe that's suitable for your skill level. Whether you're looking to trek through Desolation Wilderness in South Lake Tahoe, or you're careening towards Mount Rose's vertical and rocky terrain, for a chance to glimpse the looming view of nearby Reno and the resplendent lake waters, there's something for everyone here. If you're planning to tackle more than just Tahoe's hikes, read from our Lake Tahoe <u>Travel Guide section of this book</u> to put together the perfect itinerary.

Mount Rose: North Lake Tahoe
The hike up Mount Rose in North Lake Tahoe is epic. It's 10 miles (16 km) there-and-back of stunning wilderness and the abundant beauty of Mother Nature. This hike starts at one of the highest elevations. You'll begin at 8,900 feet (2,712 meters) and climb to 10,776 feet (3,284 meters), and looms over Reno and the resplendent waters of stunning Lake Tahoe.

You'll discover this hike off Highway 431. At the peak of this trail, you'll discover spellbinding views that seemingly stretch on forever. From Reno and Carson City to Sparks, Boca and the Tahoe Basin, you'll see it all in full glory. From Alpine forest at the basin up towards sharp and jagged cliffs with protruding granite rocks, the steep elevation changes in this trail make it one of the more difficult ones to climb.

Mount Tallac: South Lake Tahoe

Somewhere between Emerald Bay and Camp Richardson, you'll discover the trailhead that leads you to the day-long hike up Mount Tallac. This 9.5 mile (15.2 km) there-and-back of trails provides awe-inspiring views of the Alpine forests and Desolation Wilderness. Gaze out towards the sparkling azure-hued waters of Lake Tahoe in this fairly intense hike.

You can pick up a free permit for the hike in the Desolation Wilderness area. On your way to the trailhead, you'll find a well-signed road after you turn onto Mount Tallac Road. Captivating views at the top reveal Emerald Bay in all its glory along with Cascade and Fallen Leaf Lakes. You'll be mesmerized as the scenery changes from the Tahoe Lake Basin up towards granite cliffs and ridges at an elevation gain of 3,500 feet (1,066 meters) at the peak of the hike from its base.

Echo Lake to Ralston Lake: South Lake Tahoe

The Echo Lake to Ralston Lake trail in South Lake Tahoe sits between two peaks. The Echo Peak and the Ralston Peak tower above with the water resting majestically in the valley between. This provides incredible terrain through the Desolation Wilderness for hiking of approximately 6.5 miles (10.4 km) of Alpine forest and glacier-carved granite cliffs.

The hike is moderate. You'll climb approximately 1,200 feet (365.7 meters) during the jaunt. Close to the topic, you'll enjoy epic views, not only of the two lakes, but also of Lake Tahoe's shimmering blue waters in the distance. You'll find the trailhead located near Spooner Summit parking lot just off Highway 50.

Eagle Falls & Eagle Lake Trail: South Lake Tahoe

Eagle Falls and Eagle Lake Trail is located in South Lake Tahoe. Just look for Vikingsholm Castle in Emerald Bay and simply follow the road into Desolation Wilderness from there towards Eagle Falls Trailhead. The hike is mild. That might be why it's popular. It's a 2 mile (3.2 km) round trip scenic beauty that includes sweeping views of sparkling Emerald Bay.

From this trail, you can discover additional hiking. Venture off towards Desolation Wilderness. Or, stay on the not-so-straight-and-narrow trail towards Eagle Falls and back down to Vikingsholm Castle on the beach. It's a truly epic hike with breathtaking views of the surrounding snow-capped mountains and deep-hued resplendent waters of Lake Tahoe.

Spooner to Marlette Lake: Glenbrook

This hike is located close to Sand Harbor along the northeastern coast of Lake Tahoe, on the Nevada side. Marlette Lake offers a heavenly reprieve into the Alpine forests and glacier-carved granite cliffs that engulf the area. Blue skies and the warmth of the summer sun offers the perfect backdrop for a hike that originates at Spooner Lake.

In total, you'll trek 9.5 miles (15.2 km) round trip, to and fro. Look for the parking lot at Spooner Lake and locate the North Canyon Trail, which offers a gradual incline of a meer 1,200 feet (365.7 meters). Marlette is ideal for picnics, especially during the warm summer months. You'll also enjoy blissful panoramic views of Lake Tahoe near the top.

Lola Montez Lakes Trail: North Lake Tahoe
Popular with mountain bikers, the Lola Montez Lakes trail in North Lake Tahoe is a great hike if you're simply looking for an arduous trek through the woods. However, don't expect any commanding views of Lake Tahoe from this hiking trail. Still, you will get to enjoy Mother Nature at its finest along with babbling creeks and granite cliffs and deep Alpine forests along the way.

This hike is roughly 6.5 miles (10.4 km) with approximately 2,300 feet (701 meters) gained in elevation along the way. The Lola Montez Lake is great for swimming, especially in the summer. Although you won't see any of Lake Tahoe, you will enjoy blissful views of Lola Montez

Lake. To access this trail, you'll take the Soda Springs exit from Highway 80. There's a paved road that you can find on the northern end of the freeway after the fire station.

Tahoe Meadows Interpretive Trail: North Lake Tahoe

If you're looking for a less arduous and much less stressful hike, then the Tahoe Meadows Interpretive Trail in North Lake Tahoe is for you. You can find this trail in Incline Village off Highway 431 at the 28/431 interchange. You'll head up the hill towards the summit where you'll see signs directing you toward the trail.

You won't have much of an incline on this trail, but you'll start at a higher elevation at around 8,740 feet (2,663 meters) and the entire journey is roughly 1.2 miles round trip. Not very much when you compare it some of the other hikes and trails you can find in the Lake Tahoe area.

Rubicon Trail: West Shore

The Rubicon Trail on Lake Tahoe's west shore follows the shoreline of the lake. It's one of the only trails to do so. While easy, it is long. On the way, engulf the senses in captivating views of the shimmering lake waters. Winding along the shore, you'll also discover coves along the way for swimming. Cool off in the crystal-clear waters during those sun-soaked summer days.

There's not much of a change in elevation on this hike. You'll start at 6,240 feet (1,901 meters) and go up to 6,624 feet (2,018 meters). The route is 12.3 miles (19.7 km) and it rounds around Emerald Bay and up through D.L. Bliss State Park. You can find the trailhead at the southern end of the Emerald Bay Boat-In Campground

Lake Tahoe 4th Of July Independent Day

To give you an idea of what to expect, here's a quick rundown of last year's celebration.

10:00am - Who doesn't love a parade? The kids most certainly do. Begin your Tahoe Independence Day celebration with their signature *4th of July Parade* in South Lake Tahoe. Beginning at the "Y" where Highways 89 and 50 intersect and ending at Bijou Community Park, this annual cascade of cachet doubles as a fundraiser for the American Legion, and concludes with a communal BBQ held immediately afterwards in the park.

10:00am to 5:00pm - For more prolonged revelers, it's difficult to compete with the all-day beach party that is *Fun on the Beach at Zephyr Cove*. And with a DJ starting at 11am as well as adult beverages offered soon thereafter, near the water is the place to be for your Lake Tahoe 4th of July celebration. Parking for Zephyr Cove opens at 6am and does fill up fast, as even on normal summer days Zephyr Cove is one of the more popular beaches in Tahoe. It should also be noted that while families do frequent this beach, this particular event is not recommended for younger children, especially later in the day.

6:00pm to 8:30pm - Hungry for a little more BBQ? Of course you are. It's the 4th of July in Tahoe after all, and the _BBQ at the Beach Retreat & Lodge_ should satisfy every hungry traveler under their beachfront tent. Adults and children are always welcomed, and guests can watch the fireworks from the beach with their bellies now properly full.

7:00pm - Looking for a more refined and sophisticated way to spend your Fourth in Lake Tahoe? Perhaps one of Lake Tahoe's _July 4th Fireworks Cruises_ is more your speed. Both the MS Dixie and Tahoe Paradise offer exquisite cruise underneath the fireworks filling the sky. The MS Dixie includes dinner, dancing, live entertainment and spectacular views of the fireworks, while the Tahoe Paradise offers a more modest spread that includes mainly appetizers. Due to their overwhelming popularity, the tickets are pricey, but well worth every penny. With the unrivaled and unobstructed views available from the center of the lake, it's an experience unlike anything else.

9:45pm - Of course, some would argue that there is no such thing as a bad view of _Lights on the Lake Fireworks_. And they would have a point, as the show can be seen from basically anywhere in town and has been frequently rated as one of the top 5 firework shows in the country. Just be sure to have a radio nearby, as there is an accompanying soundtrack you can follow along to by tuning your radio to a specific station. It truly is music to your ears!

Lake Tahoe Ski Guide & Resorts

Lake Tahoe is one of the world's ultimate ski destinations. In fact, it's likely one of the world's most diverse. Due to its higher elevations and the fact that it straddles the Sierra Nevada mountains, summers are warm and dry while winters offer the quietude and solace of a snowy winter wonderland. If you're heading to Tahoe for its world-famous skiing, check out our guide below. Or, take a look at our _Lake Tahoe travel guide_ page for a complete list of all there is to do in Lake Tahoe, no matter what time of year you go.

South Lake Tahoe Ski Resorts

Heavenly Mountain Resort (California) - 6567 ft base (2001 meters), 10067 ft (3068 meters) summit - Longest run is 5.5 miles (8.85 km) and biggest vertical drop is 3502 ft (1067 meters)

Kirkwood (California) - 7800 ft base (2377 meters), 9800 ft summit (2987 meters) - Longest run is 2.5 miles (4.02 km) and biggest vertical drop is 2000 ft (609 meters)

Sierra-at-Tahoe (California) - 6640 ft (2023 meters) base, 8852 ft (2698 meters) summit - Longest run is 2.5 miles (4.02 km) and biggest vertical drop is 2212 ft (674 meters)

North Lake Tahoe Ski Resorts

Boreal Mountain Resort (California) - 7200 ft base (2194 meters), 10067 ft (3068 meters) summit - Longest run is 1 miles (1.6 km) and biggest vertical drop is 500 ft (152 meters)

Diamond Peak (Nevada) - 6700 ft base (2042 meters), 8540 ft (2603 meters) summit - Longest run is 2.5 miles (4.02 km) and biggest vertical drop is 1840 ft (560 meters)

Donner Ski Ranch (California) - 7031 ft base (2143 meters), 8012 ft (2442 meters) summit - Longest run is 1.5 miles (2.41 km) and biggest vertical drop is 750 ft (228 meters)

Homewood Mountain Resort (California) - 6230 ft base (1898 meters), 7880 ft (2401 meters) summit - Longest run is 2.0 miles (3.21 km) and biggest vertical drop is 1650 ft (502 meters)

Mt. Rose - Ski Tahoe (Nevada) - 8260 ft base (2517 meters), 9700 ft (2956 meters) summit - Longest run is 2.5 miles (4.02 km) and biggest vertical drop is 1800 ft (548 meters)

Northstar California (California) - 6330 ft base (1929 meters), 8610 ft (2624 meters) summit - Longest run is 1.4 miles (2.25 km) and biggest vertical drop is 2280 ft (694 meters)

Squaw Valley - Alpine Meadows (California) - 6200 ft base (1889 meters), 9050 ft (2758 meters) summit - Longest run is 3.2 miles (5.15 km) and biggest vertical drop is 2850 ft (868 meters)

Soda Springs (California) - 6700 ft base (2042 meters), 7352 ft (2240 meters) summit - Longest run is 0.4 miles (0.64 km) and biggest vertical drop is 652 ft (198 meters)

Sugar Bowl Resort (California) - 6883 ft base (2097 meters), 8383 ft (2555 meters) summit - Longest run is 3.0 miles (4.82 km) and biggest vertical drop is 1500 ft (457 meters)

Tahoe Donner (California) - 6750 ft base (2057 meters), 7350 ft (2240 meters) summit - Longest run is 1.0 miles (1.60 km) and biggest vertical drop is 600 ft (182 meters)

Lake Tahoe in the Summer

Summers in Tahoe are epic. Think long sun-soaked afternoons. Golden-sanded beaches. Pristine shorelines. In the distance snow-capped peaks that hug the circumference of the lake. Shimmering lake waters and awe-inspiring views will take your breath away, day-in and day-out.

If you're heading to Lake Tahoe in the summertime, a Utopian mecca awaits. There's *so much to do all over the entire area*. It's a time of the year when you can enjoy the resplendent lake waters and take in the intoxicating crisp mountain air. You can fish. Hike. Mountain bike. Paddleboard. Parasail. Go boating. Take a cruise. Golf. See historic sites. And so much more.

There's a reason why summers in Lake Tahoe is in one of the most sought-after destinations in the world. There's something for everyone here. No matter what you're into. Here, you'll find it. Whether it's romantic outings with a loved one. Parties on the beach with friends. Or hiking with the entire family.

However, if you're heading to Tahoe in the summer, you're likely looking to plan your itinerary. What thing can do you in Tahoe in the summer? Specifically? There are likely hundreds, if not thousands of things to do. But amidst all the potential possibilities, there are 10 things that stand out from the rest.

Hiking in Lake Tahoe in The Summer
Hiking is a great way to connect with Mother Nature. From epic day-long trips to quick strolls and jaunts, Tahoe has it all. The Lake Tahoe basin is surrounded by mountains around all sides. They hug and straddle the resplendent lake. No matter what direction you travel, you'll be met with spellbinding views that will take your breath away.

If you're heading to Lake Tahoe in the summer, you should definitely consider hiking some of its trails. From granite cliffs to hillsides blanketed with Fir and Pine trees. There is unmatched beauty here. It allows for reflection. For deep thought. For recharging your batteries. An exhilarating way to get inspired and motivated for the next chapter in life.

There are loads of epic hikes in Lake Tahoe. Not just challenging ones. You'll also find hikes that are perfect for the entire family. Not only can you hike the circumference of the lake and its surrounding hillsides, but also towards smaller finger lakes like Eagle Lake, Lake Kirkwood, Lily Pond Lake, Lower Echo Lake, Spooner Lake and more.

Fishing in Lake Tahoe in The Summer
From fishing in Lake Tahoe to fly fishing in Donner Lake, summer in Lake Tahoe presents abundant opportunities to fish the fresh waters. From the Truckee River and beyond, you can find opportunities to fish. However, take caution. The water is cold and moves fast in some areas. Be safe, no matter what lake or river you decide to fish in.

Lake Tahoe is home to a diverse species of fish that would wet the appetite of the avid fisher. Here, not only will you find Rainbow Trout, but also Brown Trout, Kokanee Salmon, Mosquito Fish, Largemouth and Smallmouth Bass, Sockeye Salmon, Golden Shiner, Mountain Whitefish, Brown Bullhead and more.

However, please note that you can't just come to Lake Tahoe and fish. First, you have to be at least 16-years old. Plus, you need to have a valid sport fishing license for California or Nevada in order to be eligible to fish in Lake Tahoe. If you're looking to fish in any of the small finger lakes or streams that surround Lake Tahoe, you'll need a license for the state that its located in.

Biking in Lake Tahoe in The Summer

Biking the circumference of the lake and its 72 miles of idyllic landscape and scenery is quite possibly one of the most soul-quenching activities you can do in the summer in Lake Tahoe. But you can do more than just bike the lake's circumference. You can also mountain bike. In fact, Northstar Resort, in North Lake Tahoe, has a chairlift just for mountain biking.

The *Northstar mountain biking park* offers 125 miles of both scenic and grueling mountain biking. Situated at an elevation of 7,899 feet, you'll find 2 chairlifts in operation here. You can rent gear and bikes if you don't have your own. And, you'll encounter everything from easy fire roads to advanced downhills with epic drops and treacherous rock gardens.

Of course, there's more biking in Lake Tahoe in the summer. In the south, you'll discover a bike path. This paved trail goes through Camp Richardson. It also passes several popular beaches along the way. From Pope Beach to Baldwin Beach and Kiva Beach. It's a scenic tour that will leave you mesmerized.

There's also the Flume Trail. Elevations here vary between 7,000 feet and 8,100 feet. It heads over Lake Tahoe's east shore. With moderate difficulty, you'll be met with more sweeping views on this mountain biking trail. There's also the Tahoe Rim Trail. It offers approximately 165 miles of epic (sometimes advanced) trails, with parts of it being off limits near Desolation, the Mount Rose Wilderness Area, and Granite Chief.

Beaches in Lake Tahoe in The Summer

Lake Tahoe boasts epic golden-sanded beaches and secluded coves that lend way to the resplendent fresh waters of the lake. There are numerous beaches you can enjoy in the spring and summer. However, come early. Especially during peak months. The beaches fill up fast with tourists who flock to Lake Tahoe for its summer fun.

Lake Tahoe in April

Lake Tahoe in April is a haven for travelers looking to avoid the crowds. It's a time when resorts are still open for skiing. The days are longer and the nights shorter. From the beginning of April through to the end of the month, the length of the day increases dramatically. In fact, it goes up by 1 hour and 9 minutes, which equates to roughly 2 minutes and 23 seconds per day more of daylight per day.

A time when you accommodation rates are low and the options for things to do are abundant. The spring brings warmer weather in April.

But not by much. Expect the temperatures to hover around freezing at 32 °F (0 °C) and the low rarely dipping below 18 °F (-7.77 °C) and the high rarely exceeding 39 °F (3.88 °C).

While the temperature is still too cold to dip in the lake, on a warm sunny day, head over to the golden sands of one of Lake Tahoe's fabled beaches. Hit the shores of Sand Harbor towards the north shore or head down south towards Emerald Bay Beach where you can catch glimpses of Fannette Island and tour the Vikingsholm Castle.

Lake Tahoe in May

Lake Tahoe in May signals the very late spring and very beginnings of an early summer. But, be prepared for varying temperatures. While some years might be seasonally warm during May in Tahoe, with potentially 70 °F (21.1 °C) weather other years might still see snowfall during the same month.

Although you won't score the same deals you would in April, most *Lake Tahoe cabins and condos* are still at a considerable discount to what you'll pay come high season in July and August through to September. You can likely still find some deals. Especially if you book last minute. Considering it's not a very busy season, there's good likelihood you can score something good at a great price.

You can find all sorts of things to do in Lake Tahoe in May. From hiking the various trails to hanging out on the golden sands of one of its blissful beaches, Lake Tahoe is a haven in May. Crisp temperatures that aren't too cold, and definitely not too hot, will have you outdoors exploring the epic beauty of this incredible destination.

Lake Tahoe in June

June in Lake Tahoe beckons the high season. It's a time when visitors flock to the golden sands and Alpine forests of this stunning destination. In June, expect to pay more for just about everything. And, expect to deal with crowds. If you're looking to hit the beaches in Lake Tahoe, definitely plan on arriving early.

In June, the weather in Lake Tahoe will typically range from anywhere as low as 34 °F (1.11 °C) to 77 °F (25 °C). The weather is never too hot. And the lake is still cool. While you can definitely enjoy the lake, the waters will be colder, even in June. However, this does present some of the best weather for enjoying hikes in and around the Lake Tahoe area.

Lake Tahoe in July

Lake Tahoe in July is peak high season. Expect to pay more. A lot more. For everything. And, expect crowds. July and August are by far the busiest summer months in Lake Tahoe. Everything is crowded. For July, it's definitely recommended that you book your Tahoe cabin or condo early. As early as possible. Especially if you want to snag your first choice of where to stay.

The *beaches in Lake Tahoe* are teeming with tourists in July. With temperatures in the range of 40 °F (5.55 °C) to 82 °F (27.7 °C). In July, you'll also find the 4th of July Parade in Downtown Truckee along with the Lake Tahoe Shakespeare Festival. July is also a great month for just about anything outdoorsy. Golf, jet ski, go hiking, or whatever else floats your boat. This is the month to do all of that.

Lake Tahoe in August

August in Lake Tahoe is also teeming with visitors. The shores and beaches are packed. So are the hiking trails and accommodations. Getting a golf tee time is more challenging in August as well. For those that are into mountain biking, the Truckee Mountain Bike Park is also packed full of people. The weather is warm and people are enjoying the awe-inspiring beauty of Lake Tahoe in its full glory in August.

During the month of August, you can expect temperatures that range anywhere from 38 °F (3.33 °C) to 87 °F (30.55 °C). You'll have your pick of things to do in Lake Tahoe August. Everything outdoors related is entirely up for grabs. Plus, you'll get to be in the outdoors, in a breathtaking destination that includes towering Alpine forests that spiral into the heavens and glacier-carved granite cliffs that will leave you speechless.

Lake Tahoe in September

September in Lake Tahoe is still packed. You might not have the fierce crowds of the peak months in July and August, but you'll still be competing for real estate on the golden sands and rocky shores of most beaches in Lake Tahoe. September is a serene month. The air cools a bit. But not by much. You still have access to everything outdoor related in a cooler temperature.

In September, you can expect temperatures to range from 38 °F (3.33 °C) to 78 °F (30.55 °C) in Lake Tahoe. Accommodation prices drop a bit. But not by much. You'll still expect to pay those higher summer rates for any cabins or condos you rent in either North Lake Tahoe or South Lake Tahoe.

Lake Tahoe in October

October really is the tail end of summer in Lake Tahoe. If you can even call it that. However, it's a time when the crowds have relatively died down. Don't expect to pay as much for accommodation in Lake Tahoe. Those pricey cabins and condos aren't quite filled during this time of the year, so you'll have your pick.

This really is a transition month. Although crowds are still here, it's nothing compared to the peak summer months that descend on Lake Tahoe in say July and August. Prices are lower, along with wait times for just about anything. Whether you're dining or heading to the beaches for the view, it's a great time to spend at the end of summer in Lake Tahoe if you're looking to avoid the crowds.

Lake Tahoe Recreation

North Lake Tahoe Recreation

No matter the season, there are tons of North Lake Tahoe recreation and adventure to be had . Winter weather brings world class *ski resorts*, snowmobiling, *cross country skiing*, snow shoeing and more. Families love the snowparks with their *sledding and tubing* hills. Go *ice skating* with that special someone or take advantage of the many businesses that offer *snowboard and ski rentals*.

North Lake Tahoe summer recreation offers a whole different kind of adventure with beaches galore where you can sunbathe and swim. Professional Lake Tahoe businesses offer watercraft and *boat rentals*, boat cruises, and tour guides. *Rent a bike* and explore hundreds of trails, charter a fishing expedition and catch the biggest fish in the lake, or take the family to your favorite *camping and RV park*.

Challenging *golf courses* offer the chance to compete with friends and improve your game. *North Lake Tahoe hiking trails* lead to amazing views of the lake and surrounding mountains, and can be explored on foot, mountain bike, or *horseback*. When you are all tuckered out, relax in a spa and enjoy a massage. North Lake Tahoe is full of opportunities to do just about anything, allowing you to create memories that will last a lifetime.

Winter Recreation
Adventures and Tours

Your vacation isn't complete until you've experienced a Lake Tahoe guided outdoor adventure! Grab an oar and navigate white water rapids on a thrilling Truckee River rafting tour. Lace up those boots and hit the hiking trails with an experienced guide. Feel your heart pump in your chest on one of the thrilling Lake Tahoe helicopter tours. For the more faint-at-heart, a bus tour around the lake will be adventure enough. With so many ways to tour Lake Tahoe, it's hard to know where to start. Here are a few of our favorites!

Prepare to get splashed when you book a whitewater rafting trip with Tributary Whitewater Tours. Navigating rivers such as the Truckee, American, Yuba, and Carson is easy with a highly-trained guide who will give you a fun-filled and unforgettable adventure. The Lake Tahoe Adventure Company will set you up with an exhilarating kayaking trip, a mountain biking escapade, hiking expedition, guided rock climbing trip, or a combination of two or three of these for a multi-sport experience.

Get an overhead view of Lake Tahoe attractions from the jump-seat of a whirlybird provided by Sierra Air Helicopter Tours. Squaw Valley High

Camp is an adventure the whole family will love, starting with panoramic views of Lake Tahoe. You can also test your rock climbing abilities, show off your ice skating skills, slip and slide down the snow tubing hill, take a dunk in the swimming lagoon or relax in the spa. Lake Tahoe adventures are abundant and will add a thrill to your vacation that will create memories to last a lifetime. Book your Lake Tahoe adventure today!

Lake Tahoe Ski Packages
Serving the Greater Lake Tahoe Area. CA
From lodging to lift tickets to Lake cruises, find everything you need to make your next Lake Tahoe adventure a great success. With hotels and resorts ranging from the North to the South and everywhere in between, a variety of skiing options including lift tickets to individual resorts or an interchangeable booklet to seven great resorts and an abundance of things to do off the slopes, Vacations Made Easy is your winter fun planning destination. Contact us today for great deals on Lake Tahoe Ski Packages.

Discover Lake Tahoe, Inc.
Serving the Greater Lake Tahoe Area.South Lake Tahoe, CA 96150
Discover Lake Tahoe, Inc. is Lake Tahoe's premier tour provider offering tours year round. They are a locally owned tour / charter shuttle bus company serving Lake Tahoe and the Sierra as well as northern California and Nevada. They offer regularly scheduled

sightseeing tours throughout the Lake Tahoe area. They specialize in Lake Tahoe sightseeing tours for individuals, small groups and private charters in their modern, state of the art shuttle buses equipped with flat screen TV, DVD player, AC, air ride suspension, reclining seats and more. Discover Lake Tahoe is dedicated to getting you and your group to their final destination safely, comfortably and on time.

Granlibakken Treetop Adventure Park
725 Granlibakken Rd. Tahoe City, CA 96145
High in the trees of the Granlibakken Resort, near Tahoe's North shore, stands the spectacular "Tahoe Treetop Adventure Park." This park features 65 tree platforms connected by bridges, zip lines, logs, swings, and more. Some obstacles are easy, while others are more difficult to cross, but they're all extremely fun!

Regardless of age or skill level, Treetop Adventure Park has something for everyone. The park has two separate sections "The Flying Squirrel" consists of 3 different courses for beginners and children ages 5+. Ranging from beginner to advanced, young kids of all ages will have fun playing in the trees. All children and teens are required to have an adult present for the entire 2.5 hour session.

The Monkey Course offers 5 different areas for older, advanced kids and adults. You must be a minimum of 4'8" (56 inches, 142cm) to use the Monkey Course. These courses also range from beginner to advanced, so everyone participating will have a great experience climbing through the trees. Although the advanced rope course can be challenging, it's also intensely fun and very satisfying to complete, especially with the ending obstacle being a 300' zip line ride down to the forest floor!

If you'd rather keep your feet on the ground, it's easy to relax at Treetop Adventure Park. Enjoy the shady, comfortable environment while watching family and friends take on the obstacles above. You will probably leave a bit dusty, so leave your nice clothes and shoes at home. The instructors are all very friendly, focused on guest enjoyment, and they'll help everyone with their harnesses, making sure all participants understood how the safety clips work. The Treetop Adventure Park also offers team building exercises and does a great job of making everyone feel welcome while having fun.

Reservations for the daily sessions are highly recommended and fill up far in advance, so grab your spot days in advance!

High Sierra Water Ski School
1850 West Lake Blvd. Tahoe City, CA 96145
High Sierra Water Ski School offers two convenient locations to serve you one at the Sunnyside Restaurant, Lodge & Marina and the second on the West Shore at the Homewood High & Dry Marina. They offer water skiing and wakeboard lessons, boat rentals, boat charters, jet ski

rentals, along with canoe, kayak and equipment rentals. High Sierra Water Ski School invites you to experience Lake Tahoe's most fun and exciting summer recreation operation, perfect for family boat trips and summer vacation activities.

Sierra Air Helicopters
10356 Truckee Airport Rd. Truckee, CA 96161
When you book a tour with Sierra Air Helicopters, you're not just getting a helicopter ride, you're getting one of the best guided tours Lake Tahoe has to offer. Sierra Air Helicopters have many tour options to choose from whether you request a15 minute flight over the North Shore or a one hour guided tour around Lake Tahoe. Enjoy the spectacular views of Lake Tahoe and the surrounding landscape only like you can from the air. Let the knowledgeable pilot guide you over the wondrous sights that only Lake Tahoe affords.

Squaw Valley Adventure Center
1960 Squaw Valley Rd. Olympic Valley, CA 96146
Squaw Valley Adventure Center offers fun, active learning experiences for groups and individuals of all ages with challenge rope courses, indoor climbing wall and orienteering courses. Their activities include miniature golf, a ropes course, skyjump bungee trampoline, and climbing wall. Squaw Valley Adventure Center's group programs introduce a challenge and the opportunity for personal discovery, group awareness and change, and lasting empowerment. Programs

may utilize the activities above and/or may include hiking, snowshoeing, orienteering (map & compass), and more! Programs can be conducted indoors or outdoors, any season.

Squaw Valley High Camp
1960 Squaw Valley Rd. Olympic Valley, CA 96146
Fun. Fun. Fun! Located at the top of Squaw Valley is Squaw Valley High Camp where you can take in uninterrupted views of Lake Tahoe and the high Sierra Mountains. Come and enjoy a day spent ice skating, rock climbing wall, snow tubing or swimming in the Swimming Lagoon. Enjoy numerous sundecks, poolside Umbrella Bar and Terrace restaurant overlooking the gorgeous mountains and Lake Tahoe. Some activities are seasonal so be sure to call for additional information on what is available during your visit. Come soak in the sun and enjoy a day 8200' above sea level.

Tahoe Adventure Company
7010 N. Lake Blvd.Tahoe Vista, CA 96148
The Tahoe Adventure Company offers unsurpassed options for a full day of Lake Tahoe exploring. They offer a wide range of adventures and specialize in combining sports to allow you to get the most out of your day. Day trips include all equipment, natural and human history as well as van shuttle when necessary. Most of their staff members are long time locals in the lake Tahoe area and offer local insight on secret spots and little known lore and history. Choose from a long list

of adventures including: Lake Tahoe Kayaking Trips, Kayaking and Mountain Biking Multi Sport, Mountain Biking Options, Hiking and Biking Multi Sport, Guided Rock Climbing, Custom Plan Your Adventure!

Tahoe Galactic Tours
South Lake Tahoe, CA 96150
Tahoe Galactic Tours is pleased to offer you a personalized and custom astronomy experience. Your tour begins with an overview of the constellations in the night sky led by one of our knowledgeable tour guides using a high-power laser pointer and concludes with viewings of various celestial objects with our powerful telescopes. Scheduled Tours for Mondays thru Saturdays. Different celestial objects are visible at different times of the year, so come back for sky tours periodically.

Tributary Whitewater Tours
10068 Hirschdale Rd. Truckee, CA 96161
Whitewater rafting trips near Lake Tahoe, from 1/2 day 3+ days on the Truckee, American, Yuba, Carson and other rivers. For all levels, from family vacation trips suitable for kids from 4 years, to rafting adventures for the expert. Reliable water flows all summer long!! Over 30 years of safe fun trips on many California rivers. List of nearby and Northern California tours:

Truckee River Raft Co.

55 West Lake Blvd. Tahoe City, CA 96145

River rafting on the Truckee is an exciting, yet safe way for a family or friends to enjoy a morning or afternoon together. A great 2-3 hours in which you enjoy a leisurely, self guided, 5- mile float on the Truckee River from Tahoe City to the River Ranch Bar, Restaurant & Hotel. Truckee River Raft Co. are the only rafting concession that exits directly into the River Ranch landing. Have lunch, drinks or just enjoy the view. You can catch a free shuttle bus back to your car at anytime until 6 p.m. daily. Truckee River Raft Co. operates daily June through September.

Cross Country Skiing

If cross country skiing is your winter sport of choice then look no further then Royal Gorge, North America's largest cross country ski resort. They have the most diverse trail system that stretches over 93 miles. You will be in awe at the most spectacular views of Lake Tahoe. At Squaw Creek Nordic Center snowshoe or cross country ski over 400 acres meticulously groomed that venture through picturesque Squaw Valley meadow. You will find many of the North Lake Tahoe ski resorts also provide amazing groomed trails through tall pines and scenic meadows. For an exhilarating change of pace book one of their moonlight snowshoeing tours exploring the peaceful and serene mountain setting by the glow of the moon.

Northstar Cross Country Telemark & Snowshoe Center

5001 Northstar Drive. Truckee, CA 96161

A cross country skiers paradise at an elevation of 7,000 feet, Northstar at Tahoe is home to more than 20 scenic trails that are 20-feet wide in most spots. At the Northstar Cross Country Telemark & Snowshoe Center you will find a good mix of terrain, with eight novice trails, nine intermediate trails, and three advanced trails. Warming huts dot the area, and offer hot chocolate, hot tea, and picnic tables. The more than 35 km of trails are meticulously groomed.

The Center offers state-of-the-art equipment rentals, a sundeck, fire pits, and a large teaching area. It is located mid-mountain right next to the Vista Express Quad chairlift and can be reached using the Big Springs Gondola. Visitors with their own equipment and trail pass can use the Village Express Chairlift for direct access to the trail system. Northstar Cross Country Telemark & Snowshoe Center is not dog friendly.

Resort at Squaw Creek Nordic Center

400 Squaw Creek Road. Olympic Valley, CA 96146

Defined by its stunning scenic trails, the Resort at Squaw Creek Nordic Center is a great base camp for cross country skiing and snowshoeing. The majority of the 18 kilometers (400+ acres) of trails are gentle enough for beginners, making this a great place to learn to ski. Trails are groomed daily and wind through a serene meadow and an area full of hills.

The Resort at Squaw Creek Nordic Center combines cross country skiing and snowshoeing with a complete resort experience. You can expect luxurious accommodations at The Resort at Squaw Creek, delicious dining options, a full-service spa, refreshing pool and soothing hot tub. It offers classic and skate equipment rentals, and ski lessons for all ages. The resort sits next to Squaw Valley USA. It is not dog friendly.

North Lake Tahoe provides a variety of cross country skiing trails. Discover the many other great North Lake Tahoe cross country skiing areas near you get out and enjoy Mother Nature at it's best.

Royal Gorge Cross Country Resort
9411 Pahatsi Road. Soda Springs, CA 95728
Royal Gorge Cross Country Ski Resort is known world-wide for their iconic 200+ kilometer trail system traversing 6,000 acres of pristine forest terrain atop Donner Summit. When in full swing the Royal Gorge Cross Country Resort is grooming 7 days a week and offers full ski rentals, expert lessons and cross country ski instruction across one of the most extensive, varied, and gorgeous trail systems anywhere! Royal Gorge Cross Country Resort is now offering designated dog-friendly trails and passes, as well as a new trail system connecting

Sugar Bowl Resort and Royal Gorge's Summit Station through which traverses the beautiful Van Norden meadows. For those who can't get enough winter beauty and exercise you can buy annual passes for yourself and you dog. Come discover the winter wonderland at the Royal Gorge Cross Country Ski Resort.

Sugar Pine Point State Park
Just south of Tahoma. Tahoma, CA 96142
Bordering Lake Tahoe for almost two miles, Sugar Pine Point State Park is the largest state park at Lake Tahoe. Explore its 2,000 acres filled with sugar pine, aspen, juniper, and fir forests, plus 3.5 miles that extends into the Desolation Wilderness Area. Discover beachfront trails, gorgeous hikes, campground, swimming holes, and boating opportunities. Reconnect with the past at the Hellman-Ehrman Mansion, an early 1900s summer retreat. Take the challenge of fishing for Mackinaw, Kokanee Salmon, and Rainbow Trout.

Location, Fees, and Operating Hours
Sugar Pine Point State Park can be found on the west shore of Lake Tahoe just 10 miles south of Tahoe City, CA, on Highway 89.

The Day Use Annual Pass is accepted here, and you can expect day-use parking fees to start around $8. For camping fees and park hours call the park office at (530) 525-7982.

The Hellman-Ehrman Mansion is open from Memorial Day weekend through Labor Day. For current tour times and ticket prices call (530) 525-7232.

Activities and Adventures

Sugar Pine Point State Park is meant to be explored and discovered! You can grab a map and head out on your own, or take advantage of guide services and programs.

Start your summer adventure at the Nature Center and Gift Shop, located in the Tank House and open daily from June to the end of August, plus weekends in September. Immerse yourself in the region's geology and natural history with hands-on exhibits, interpretive displays, and an educational theater. This is also the place to get recreational guides and books.

Walk on the Dolder Nature Trail, which circles the Edwin L. Z'berg Natural Preserve and other easy nature trails. Check out the Junior Ranger Program for children between the ages 7 to 12. This summer program is led by the park staff and offers wonderful activities that foster an appreciation of our cultural and natural heritage. The park has many Hiking and Nature Trails that can be explored on your own with an informative brochure, or with a live guide in the spring, summer, and fall when staff is available. Overnight adventurists head to the General Creek Campground with its 175 sites that are open year-round.

Summer Fun!

Sugar Pine State Park's beachfront encompasses 7,000 feet. Enjoy swimming and fishing at the pier. Gently sloping lawns shaded by towering trees provide the perfect lakeside picnic spot. Bicyclists love to ride the West Shore Bike Trail. Play a game of tennis on the Hellman-Ehrman Mansion's tennis court, or tour the Pine Lodge's two boathouses to see the boats that helped start Lake Tahoe boating events. Boaters can launch, moor, and rent boats at nearby marinas, such as Obexer's Boat Company, located in Homewood. Unfortunately, boats cannot be beached or moored overnight at Sugar Pine Point State Park due to space limitations. Within just a few miles drive are other great Lake Tahoe beaches you might want to check out while visiting the area.

Love camping? Then book your next campsite at General Creek Campground, one of the largest in the Lake Tahoe basin. The scenic forest setting, paved roads, bike path, hiking trails and campground amenities make this an ideal Lake Tahoe campground.

Snow Activities

Wintertime brings a whole different kind of exploration with Guided Cross Country Ski/Snowshoe Excursions. Beginner and intermediate cross country skiers enjoy the easy terrain at Sugar Pine Point State Park. With 18.7 kilometers to explore, you will discover five color-coded trails that range from one to three miles in length. Sugar Pine is rich in Olympic history. Yes, you heard it right, the VIII Winter Olympics were held here in 1960. Check out the General Creek Trail, which takes you to the center of where the men's events took place. The biathlon as well as the men's cross country events were held here.

Activity schedules and interpretive guides are available online or by calling the park office (530) 525-7982 (snow phone), (530) 525-7232 (information). The two groomed cross-country ski trails can be explored on your own as well, and ski and snowshoe lessons are available on many weekends during the winter. This park is not dog friendly.

General Creek Campground is also the only site for winter camping on Lake Tahoe. There several other great cross country skiing trails and downhill ski resorts in the Lake Tahoe basin to keep you busy this winter.

Tahoe City Winter Sports Park
251 N. Lake Blvd. Tahoe City, CA 96162
Brings the kids and even your dog! Check out the new Tahoe City Winter Sports Park located at the Tahoe City Golf Course. This dog-friendly course offers cross country skiing and snowshoeing terrain,

plus equipment rentals this winter. There is even a small sledding hill for young children. The Tahoe City Golf Course Club House offers a restaurant and bar open a relaxing place to grab a bite to eat.

During the holidays, the Tahoe City Winter Sports Park will be open seven days a week, while the regular schedule is four days a week. All services are provided by Tahoe Cross Country and Duncan Golf Management.

Get you and experience the winter beauty at Lake Tahoe. Tahoe City Winter Sports Park and many other great Lake Tahoe cross country resorts are just waiting for you and your skis!

Tahoe Donner Cross Country Center
11603 Snowpeak Way. Truckee, CA 96160
Looking for world-class cross country skiing? Tahoe Donner Cross Country Center is ranked in the top five out of more than 450 cross country skiing facilities in the U.S. It offers an excellent launching point to more than 100 km of the most scenic terrain in the Lake Tahoe area. Groomed 7-days a week, it is perfect for diagonal striding, skating and snowshoeing. Challenge yourself on the peak trails, or take a more leisurely route across gentle rolling hills.

Among the Tahoe Donner Cross Country Center trail options is a 3.5 km run to the Cookhouse in the Euer Valley. The Cookhouse is available as a warming hut on the weekdays, but on weekends and holidays food is served. There are 36 km of trails in the Home Range, 30 km up the Sunrise bowl, and a 2.5 km night skiing loop available on Wednesday nights in January and February.

Tahoe Donner Cross Country Center offers all-day rentals, and group and private ski instruction. It has a Day Lodge with equipment rentals, ski maintenance, and trail passes. It also has Alder Creek Café offering delicious and fresh homemade food. There are five warming huts spread throughout the area. It is not dog friendly.

There are many Lake Tahoe cross country ski areas to choose from so the choice is yours. Where it be Tahoe Donner Cross Country Center, Royal Gorge or the North Lake Tahoe area you will be impressed with the beautiful mountain terrain.

Tahoe XC, Tahoe City
925 Country Club Drive. Tahoe City, CA 96145
Winter at Tahoe XC
Discover serene meadow trails, challenging hills, and a few thrilling downhill areas at Tahoe XC in Tahoe City. The setting is ideal for cross country skiers and snowshoeing enthusiasts of all abilities. Its 22 trails, spanning more than 65 km, sport stunning Lake Tahoe views. Nine kilometers of trails are machine groomed daily. Three warming huts offer free hot chocolate and pose as resting spots along the trails.

Tahoe XC is one of the few places in North Lake Tahoe that has dog-friendly trails. The two trails open to dogs and are groomed daily and cover 9 km. They offer PSIA certified instruction, plus rentals for skate, classic, and snowshoe, pull-behind sleds for kids (55 pounds or less), and kids gear. Grab a bite to eat at the Day Lodge Café and enjoy free WiFi. Tahoe XC is host to the start of the Great Ski Race, one of the largest cross country ski events in the western United States, and is located only three miles from the convenience of downtown Tahoe City.

Summer at Tahoe XC

Come in the summer when Tahoe Cross Country in Tahoe City offers trailhead mountain biking as well as bike rentals and more. Enjoy their convenient trailhead mountain bike rentals, food service, retail and repair shop. Tahoe Cross Country offers fantastic trails for beginner and intermediate riders, and there is also easy access to advanced terrain higher up. There is great terrain for all ages and abilities, riding or hiking.

Ice Skating

Come sharpen your ice skating skills or learn how to make a few turns for the first time at these wonder North Lake Tahoe ice skating rinks. The ice skating rink At the Village at Northstar™ is a 9,000 square foot rink where you can relax and watch the kids while warming up by the nearby fire pits. Sip coco and roast some marsh mellows. At the Olympic Ice Pavilion at Squaw Valley Resorttake in the dramatic views from their ice skating rink or go take a dip in their heated lagoon pool. Ice skating at Lake Tahoe is a great way to spend the day with your family and loved ones.

Olympic Ice Pavilion at Squaw Valley Resort
The Olympic Ice Pavilion is located at the top of the Cable Car at High Camp offering unmatched panoramic views of the Squaw Valley Meadow, Lake Tahoe and the surrounding Sierra Nevada mountains. This 100' x 200' outdoor ice skating rink is fun for the entire family. Hockey or figure skate rentals are included in the cost, and private lessons are available by appointment. The Olympic Ice Pavilion was designed to be environmentally friendly. A state-of-the-art heat exchanger freezes the ice for the rnk while simultaneously heating the water for the Swimming Lagoon & Spa, surrounding decks, and walkways as well as the High Camp Bath & Tennis Club. The Olympic Ice Pavilion is open daily throughout the High Camp winter and summer seasons. Can be reserved for large groups. Come experience great outdoor adventure on Lake Tahoe's North Shore. _Located at the top of the Cable Car at High Camp. Squaw Valley, CA 96146_

Village at Northstar Ice Rink

The Northstar Ice Rink is located in the heart of the Village at Northstar™. This 9,000 square foot ice skating rink adds to that perfect winter vacation at Northstar™. After a day on the mountain come enjoy watching the kids on the ice rink while you enjoy a hot toddy or a hot mulled cider by the outdoor fire pits. Maybe you prefer to sharpen your old ice skating skills or feel brave enough to learn a new one ice skating for the first time. In the evenings purchase a s'mores kit and savor the tasty treats with family at the fire pits. The Northstar Ice Rink hours of operation are Sunday through Thursday: 12:00 p.m. to 8:00 p.m. and Friday through Saturday: 12:00 p.m. to 9:00 p.m. weather permitting. *3001 Northstar Drive. Truckee, CA 96160*

Ski Resorts
North Lake Tahoe is home to some of the world's finest ski resorts like Squaw Valley, Alpine Meadows, and Northstar at Tahoe. These resorts see over 400 inches of pure white snow each year that attract skiers and snowboarders from all over the world. Top winter sports legends have called North Lake Tahoe home, most recently Olympic gold winner Shaun White. The top of the line amenities these resorts offer will keep you busy for days, but it's the snow that keeps you coming back. Light and fluffy snow combined with epic downhill runs, half-pipes and parks, majestic views, and crystal clear air makes for the perfect winter vacation. Oh ya, did we mention Lake Tahoe? At Lake

Tahoe recreation is virtually endless. So consider your vacation is just beginning once you are off the hill.

It's not just the large North Lake Tahoe ski resorts that draw the crowds. Smaller resorts like Homewood and Diamond Peak offer jaw-dropping views of Lake Tahoe and really cater to families. Diamond Peak has a vertical drop of 1,840 feet which make it the fourth longest drop in the Lake Tahoe area. Homewood is protected from the wind when most large resorts go on wind hold. Boreal, Sugar Bowl, Soda Springs and Tahoe Donner also bring their unique qualities to the table. Boreal Ski Resort is the first and only all-mountain terrain park in the Lake Tahoe region. Sugar Bowl is a world-class mountain resort that features four peaks and 95 runs spread out over 1,500 acres. Combine easy Interstate 80 access, more affordable rates, and plenty of snow and these resorts will easily make your list of ski resorts to explore on your next trip to Lake Tahoe. Don't forget to venture to the South Lake Tahoe ski resorts where your skiing adventure continues.

Alpine Meadows Ski Resort
2600 Alpine Meadows Road. Tahoe City, CA 96145

Alpine Meadows ski resort is recognized world-wide for its diverse terrain and spectacular Lake Tahoe views. It also offers the longest season of any Lake Tahoe ski resort with 402 inches of annual snowfall. Alpine Meadows and Squaw Valley USA now offer a combined season pass. Visitors have access to more than 6,000 acres, eight mountain peaks, 44 lifts, and over 270 trails. Each resort will maintain its individual character, which means Alpine Meadows' relaxed and easygoing atmosphere will continue to charm locals and visitors alike.

Alpine Meadows has two beautiful lodges where visitors can relax by the fireplace and get a bite to eat, one is found at the base of the resort and one at mid-mountain. The base area day lodge also offers rentals and repair, a children's ski and snowboard center, play area, six dining options, and more. A favorite activity is the Alpine Chalet Experience which includes a snow cat ride to the Mid Mountain Chalet where guests can experience a four-course gourmet dining experience.

Ski Alpine Meadows starting at an elevation of 8,637 feet; its blood-pumping advanced runs and seven open bowls, paired with gentle cruising trails give one and all a very rounded out experience. The resort's 14 lifts provide access to 100 designated runs covering 2,400 patrolled acres and three challenging terrain parks. Best of all, the Alpine Meadows web cams provide real time views of the freshest powder on the mountain. In addition, families will love the children's center, with its lessons, snow tubing, and a mini-terrain park.

Alpine Meadows is host to Lake Tahoe's only triple-air competition, the Take the Lake Triple Jump Line Competition, which takes place in the legendary Shreadows Terrain Park. Visitors can also rock the mountain at the Bandwagon, a snow grooming machine that has been converted into a mobile entertainment system that you have to see to believe. Alpine Meadows, CA, is situated just eight miles northwest of Tahoe City, California, and only 14 miles south of Truckee. The closest airport is the Reno-Tahoe International Airport, which is just 45 miles away on Interstate 80. Get your ticket and experience Alpine Meadows today!

Alpine Meadows is one of the many great Lake Tahoe ski resorts to choose from. Our Lake Tahoe ski resorts map will help you select your next ski or snowboarding destination to challenge your skills.

13 Lifts:
1 high-speed detachable six-passenger chai
2 high-speed express quad
3 triple and five double chairs
2 surface lifts (one of two surface lifts is for Kids' Camp participants only)

Season: Mid-November through late May
Hours of Operations (PST): Lodge Open Daily 8am-4pm. Lifts Open Daily 9am-4pm (wind and weather permitting)

Base Elevation: 6,835 feet

Summit Elevation: 8,637 feet

Snowmaking: Covers a network of runs served by 11 of 13 lifts, serving beginner through expert runs.

Average Annual Snowfall: 495 inches

Total Acreage: 2,400 acres

Trails: 100+ designated runs

Classification Total: 25% easier, 40% more difficult, 35% most difficult/expert

Boreal Ski Resort
19659 Boreal Ridge Rd. Truckee, CA 96161

Boreal Ski Resort is the first and only all-mountain terrain park in the Lake Tahoe region. This quaint resort offers many fun adventures compacted into its 480 acres, making it attractive to legions of snowboarders as well as families seeking an enjoyable and affordable adventure. The average snowfall is 400 inches, so you will want to check out Boreal web cams for accurate and up-to-the-minute views of mountain conditions.

With 41 trails to explore accessed by eight lifts, plus a vertical rise of 500 feet, those who ski Boreal can expect to navigate exciting tree runs and complex gullies, plus a tube park with its own magic carpet lift. The resort's three awesome terrain parks are a favorite of snowboarders and include the Superpipe. The Boreal's state-of-the-art BagJump is an amazing action sports training device that will help you perfect your next trick. This 50-by-50 foot cushion will absorb the impact of your landing with maximum softness.

Boreal's Woodward Tahoe, open to visitors summer 2012, is an action sports facility that has terrain parks and snow features for free-ride and free-ski practice. This facility offers classes and camps to improve snowboard, ski, skate, BMX, cheer, gymnastics, and film making skills. It offers year-round instruction and camp programs for any level, from beginner to advanced athletes. The indoor ski and snowboard ramps, skate park, foam pits, trampolines, digital media area, and the outdoor park and pipe area are phenomenal.

Boreal is conveniently located on Donner Summit just off Interstate 80. It is about 9 miles from Truckee, CA, 40 miles from Reno, NV, and 90 miles from Sacramento, CA. This makes it the closest Lake Tahoe ski resort to Sacramento and the Bay Area in California. You will definitely want make Boreal a part of your vacation this season.

Like so many Lake Tahoe ski resorts Boreal has a lot to offer. Expand to other local resorts with our Lake Tahoe ski resorts map. There is something unique and special at each Lake Tahoe ski resort.

Diamond Peak Ski Resort
1210 Ski Way. Incline Village, NV 89451

Lake Tahoe's Friendliest Mountain

Located in Incline Village, Nevada, Diamond Peak has a little something for everyone, although the stunning views of Lake Tahoe alone are reason enough to visit this fantastic destination. The mountain is teeming with opportunities for beginners with its gentle slopes and wide runs, while experts can experience the challenging terrain of Solitude Canyon. The summit is at an elevation of 8,540 feet and it has a vertical drop of 1,840 feet, the fourth longest drop in the Lake Tahoe area. There are 655 skiable acres that area accessed by 6 lifts, with 30 runs that include fantastic tree skiing and open glades.

Diamond Peak Ski Resort caters to families with its Bee Ferrato Child Ski Center and the affordable Interchangeable Parent's Pass. There are excellent programs available to teach you how to ski or snowboard. The Diamond Peak Terrain Park on the other hand has a plethora of features for all abilities. Expect rails, boxes, massive kickers, table tops, and a wall ride. There is also a family friendly area with low flat rails and boxes.

After a calorie burning day on the slopes, head to the base lodge for something to eat. The Food Court has appealing options, including grab-and-go items, while the Lodge Pole BBQ features succulent slow-cooked pork ribs smothered in sauce and a to-die-for beef brisket sandwich. There is also a Tahoe's Taco with its Mexican themed fare, the Loft Bar, and Phatty's freshly baked cinnamon buns, scones, chocolate chunk muffins and other sweets. Snowflake Lodge is located mid-mountain and can only be accessed by skiing or snowboarding.

The resort is located in Incline Village, Nevada, on the North Shore of Lake Tahoe, just 35 miles from Reno/Tahoe International Airport. It has an average annual snowfall of about 325 inches, so you will want to take advantage of the Diamond Peak web cams for real-time views of mountain conditions. Come experience the dynamic atmosphere of the scenic Diamond Peak Ski Resort this season!

Donner Ski Ranch
19320 Donner Pass Rd. Norden, CA 95724

Family owned and operated Donner Ski Ranch is one of the last of its kind in California. As such, it offers a relaxed and carefree atmosphere making it a favorite for family fun. Beginners enjoy it for the simple experience that it provides, and more advanced skiers and snowboarders find a lot to explore as well. With six chair lifts and two moving carpets, the terrain spans more than 500 acres and offers fast-paced winter fun for visitors of every skill level.

Donner Ski Ranch provides private or group ski/snowboard instruction in their Learn to Turn Center. They also offer ski packages that include equipment, beginner group lessons, and a beginner lift ticket all for one affordable price. Check the website for daily specials and even more savings!

Donner Ski Ranch Tubing Hill

Prepare for lots of giggles and laughs as you slide down the snow tubing hill at the Donner Ski Ranch snow park. Once you are at the bottom you can hop on a magic carpet and get whisked to the top again in no time at all. Donner Ski Ranch is located at the top of Donner Summit along historic Route 40.

Granlibakken Ski Area
725 Granlibakken Rd. Tahoe City, CA 96145

Granlibakken Resort features an intimate ski hill, perfect for beginning through intermediate skiers and snowboarders. It's a great place to avoid the crowds of larger resorts, while enjoying a day of skiing right out your back door.

A rental shop, ski school, warming hut and snack bar are also on the premises. The ski hill, ski school and snack bar are open every Friday through Sunday, every day Christmas/New Years and mid-February holidays. The rental shop, snowplay area and warming hut are open daily all season.

Snowpark: Granlibakken snow park offers an area for saucers only. Rentals available, fee charged for day use.

Beyond Granlibakken there are many great Lake Tahoe ski resorts to discover. Check out our Lake Tahoe ski resorts map and plan your ultimate winter ski vacation.

Homewood Ski Resort
5145 Westlake Blvd. Homewood, CA 96141

If you are looking for some of the best skiing and snowboarding opportunities in the Lake Tahoe region, check out Homewood Ski Resort. It spans 1,260 acres on the West Shore of Lake Tahoe, and boasts beautiful views of the lake from every slope. Loved by locals and vacationers alike, Homewood was ranked 12th in SKI Magazine's 2001 reader's poll. It has an average snowfall of about 450 inches a season and enjoys 300 sunny days a year.

Homewood ski resort's base elevation is 6,230 feet and the summit peaks at 7,880 feet and can be accessed by 8 lifts and a new high-speed quad lift called the Old Homewood Express. The 60 breathtaking runs are immaculately groomed and protected from high-ridge winds by Ellis Peak, making for some of the finest powder on earth. Ski Homewood's groomed boulevards, glade runs through old-growth forest, and trademark hidden powder stashes. There is a family snow play area, plus early-season skiing and snowboarding lessons with the guarantee that you will be skiing Homewood's signature run by the third lesson.

Homewood has two terrain parks with stunning lake views and terrain for all levels of expertise, from beginners to future X Games competitors. Lakeview Park features a variety of tables, rails, flat boxes, rollers, and bank turns. Kolby's Escape is an innovative park with skate-style features including tables, steps, boxes, slant rails, and bar rails. When you are ready for a break, head to the beautiful West Shore Café and Inn for remarkable lake-front dining. Homewood is located about an hour from Reno, NV, and about two hours from Sacramento, CA, making it a great place to head for a day trip or a relaxing vacation.

Mt. Rose Ski Resort
22222 Mt. Rose Hwy. Reno, NV 89511

Just twenty-five minutes from downtown Reno, Mt. Rose Ski Resort is North Lake Tahoe's best kept secret. Whether you are looking for a quick get-away or a longer vacation, the location of this resort makes it affordable and convenient. Starting at the regions highest base elevation of 8,260 feet, the Mt. Rose elevation soars up to 9,700 feet. The panoramic views of Lake Tahoe and Nevada from the summit will absolutely take your breath away.

Mt Rose ski resort has the capacity to introduce you to some of the best powder in the Sierra Nevada Mountains. When you jump on one of the eight ski lifts you will be propelled up 1,800 vertical feet in less than four minutes. There are 62 runs, plus terrain parks for all abilities, and The Chutes offer extreme challenge for advanced skiers and snowboarders. If you want to improve your skills, the Mt. Rose Ski and Snowboard School is a great start for beginners and has advanced lessons for those looking to tear it up in The Chutes.

Dining at Mt. Rose runs the gamut with eight restaurants, bars, and coffee shops with a variety of offerings. The 431 Sports Shop is an excellent choice for top-of-the-line mountain gear, apparel, and accessories. Mt. Rose' Winters Creek Lodge is available in the winter when you need to take a ski break, or reserve space for a special event during the summer. The setting is gorgeous and relaxed, with panoramic views of the Washoe Valley and Washoe Lake. There are a number of events and entertainment planned throughout the year, including the Santa Ski Crawl, The Chutes Best Line Challenge, and the Dummy Downhill.

The Mt. Rose, Nevada, resort is located along Mt. Rose highway and is the closest resort to Reno and its Reno/Tahoe International Airport, with daily shuttle services are available from many locations. Mt. Rose web cams are your guide to slope conditions and with more than 1,200 acres of trails on both north and east facing slopes, you are sure to have an adventure at every turn. Don't miss the opportunity to explore Mt. Rose this season.

Northstar at Tahoe Ski Resort

5001 Northstar Drive. Truckee, CA 96161

Northstar Ski Resort is a first class year-round mountain paradise located in beautiful North Lake Tahoe. With endless opportunities to enjoy some of the finest powder on the planet, a dining venue at an elevation of 8,610 feet, and so much more. A vacation at Northstar at Tahoe should be at the top of your list. A bonus is its convenient location on Highway 267, only six miles north of Lake Tahoe and six miles south of downtown Truckee.

During the winter, visitors can ski Northstar's more than 3,000 acres filled with 93 ski trails. The trails are accessed by 20 lifts, including two gondolas, making for an uphill capacity of 34,799 skiers per hour. The longest run is 1.4 miles of twists and turns that will get your adrenaline pumping, while families can take advantage of the snow tubing hill with its own lift. Northstar also features seven award-winning terrain parks designed by Snow Park Technologies (SPT) and the Northstar Terrain Park Crew. Those interested in cross-country skiing, Telemark skiing, or snowshoeing will delight in the 40 kilometers of groomed trails, plus a venue with warming huts, fire pits and picnic sites with amazing views. Northstar web cams provide real-time views of conditions on the mountain, and when the weather doesn't cooperate, the resort brings out the big guns with the largest snowmaking system in North Lake Tahoe.

Summertime pleasures are also abundant. Scenic lift rides have amazing views and take you to some of the most beautiful hikes you will ever experience. Northstar is a mountain bikers dream with more than 100 miles of trails, making it one of the largest bike parks in Northern California. Northstar California golf course is a challenging 18-hole, par 72 course designed for both men and women. The Northstar Property Owners Association Tennis Center has world class tennis facility with 10 courts available for homeowners and lodging guests. There are also many opportunities for geocaching, fly fishing, and horseback riding.

The Village at Northstar is a hub for all the activity on the mountain. It is host to more than 35 shops and restaurants to suit any taste, from equipment rentals and children's boutiques to designer shoes and fine art galleries. The paint-your-own-pottery studio, candle making shop, and bead design studios offer social activities and creative learning experiences for all ages. The Village also has a conference center, movie theaters, luxury lodging options, and special events. Other activities include a 9,000 square foot skating rink, the Apex bungy trampoline, Apex ropes challenge, and a swimming and racquet club. With so much to do, Northstar resort can turn your vacation into an amazing adventure, leaving you with memories that will last a lifetime.

Soda Springs Ski Resort

Take I-80 Exit / Soda Springs Exit. Soda Springs, CA 95728. (530) 426-3901 Main. (530) 426-1010 Snow Phone

Soda Springs ski resort is a favorite for families and beginner and intermediate skiers and snowboarders. It's base elevation is 6,700 feet, and rises to a summit elevation of 7,352 feet. Visitors can confidently explore the resort's 200 acres of patrolled terrain from two ski lifts and two surface tows. This affordable resort will give you great value for your money, plus memories that will last a lifetime.

Laying claim to the title of best snow park for kids in the Lake Tahoe region, Soda Springs caters to children of all ages with its Tube Town and Planet Kids features. Tube Town has a moving carpet and three twisty-turny tube lanes. Take a sleigh ride to Planet Kids, the place where the smallest skiers, aged eight and under, can get comfortable on the snow. It has ski and snowboard lessons, tube carousels, moving carpets, mini tubing and a volcano that can be climbed and played on. There is also a mini snowmobiling course with pint-sized snowmobiles for kids ages 6 to 12. The best part is that all the gear is provided: rental skis and snowboards, boots, and helmets. The kid-friendly coaches will teach kids how to stop, turn, and be safe on the slopes.

Soda Springs has many trails to explore for the older members of the family, too. Its rental shop will outfit the whole family with state-of-the-art ski and snowboard rentals. Soda Springs is located 10 miles west of Truckee, CA, and 45 miles west of Reno, NV, on Interstate 80, making it the closest family-focused resort to Sacramento. Avoid the crowds and be prepared for an amazing family vacation at Soda Springs

Squaw Valley Ski Resort
1960 Squaw Valley Rd. Olympic Valley, CA 96146. (800) 403-0206 Main. (530) 583-6955 Snow Phone

The legendary Squaw Valley USA ski resort attracts visitors from all over the world. As the site of the 1960 Winter Olympic Games, its world-famous terrain is filled with exciting runs for skiers and snowboarders of all levels. Picture 4,000 acres of fresh powder spanning across six mountain peaks with open bowls and shoots that will give you an adrenaline rush like you've never experienced before. You might be interested to know Squaw Valley USA and Alpine Meadows offer a combined season pass making your winter runs double the fun. The hard part is picking which resort to spend your day on the hill.

Squaw Valley ski resort's aerial cable car transports guests 2,000 vertical feet to High Camp, located at the summit where the views of Lake Tahoe are astounding. From High Camp you can hit the slopes or slide across the ice of the world's highest open-air ice rink at an elevation of 8,200 feet. Also at the summit are dining venues, sport shops, snowtubing runs, most of the beginner skiing areas, and the Olympic Museum. In the summertime enjoy mountain biking, hiking, paintball, disc golf and a swimming lagoon. In addition to the 110-person aerial cable car, the Squaw Valley gondola seats 28-passengers, add to this more than 30 lifts, including four high speed quad lifts, and Squaw Valley has an uphill capacity of 49,000 guests per hour.

At the base of the mountain is the Village at Squaw Valley, which sits at an elevation of 6,200 feet. It offers more than 30 quality restaurants and bars serving a variety of food, plus specialty wine shops, fine art galleries, rental and repair shops, and exclusive shopping opportunities. The European-style village is laid out beautifully with cozy fire pits and beautiful walkways. It has indoor and outdoor climbing walls, the Headwall Skyjump bungee trampoline, and a miniature golf course. Nearby is the 18-hole Resort at Squaw Creek Golf Course, a championship course designed by Robert Trent Jones Jr.

Be sure to pick up a Squaw Valley ski resort map, your guide to more than 170 trails, 16 bowls, and a number of terrain parks. The terrain parks and half-pipe are designed and built by Snow Park Technologies, the team that built the world's first cubed 22-foot pipe which was part of a signature Red Bull event. Squaw Valley ski resort is located on Lake Tahoe's North Shore, just off of Highway 89, between Truckee and Tahoe City. It is only 42 miles from Reno and 96 miles from Sacramento on Interstate 80. The average annual snowfall at Squaw

Valley is 450 inches, despite this the resort experiences over 300 cloudless and sunny days per year, so get your Squaw Valley season pass and start your Lake Tahoe adventure in style. Additionally, Squaw Valley web cams give visitors the advantage of planning a perfect day on the slopes

Sugar Bowl Ski Resort
629 Sugar Bowl Road. Norden, CA 95724. (530) 426-9000 Main. (530) 426-1111 Snow Phone

As one of Lake Tahoe's oldest resorts, Sugar Bowl's rich history dates back to 1939. The sport of ski racing is a big part of its past as the host of memorable events such as the famous Silver Belt race and the US National Alpine Championships. Today, this world-class mountain resort features four peaks and the opportunity to Ski Sugar Bowl's 1,500 acres with 95 trails covered in some of the most amazing powder you will ever experience. It is no wonder the locals rave about the remarkable adventures this mountain has to offer.

The elevation at the summit is 8,383 feet and there are 13 lifts to get you where you need to go, whether it is the Sugar Bowl ski park, the Switching Yard Terrain Park, or the miles of trails in between. The terrain park's boxes, rails, mini-boarder-x, and jump lines will keep you at the top of your game, no matter your level of ability, while the terrain park competitions will give you a chance to demonstrate your skills. Sugar Bowl's backcountry tours are professionally guided and give visitors a chance to participate in educational seminars, Telemark and steeps clinics, snowshoe hikes, and more. Sugar Bowl is also participating in the Rahlves Banzai Tour 2011 where skiers and snowboarders compete for cash.

Mountain amenities include the Judah Retail Shop and Village Chalet to keep you outfitted for your adventures, and the Village Lodge for a place to relax or enjoy an excellent meal with views of Mt. Disney. The Main Lodge offers fantastic views of Mt. Judah and has two dining choices, the Sierra Vista Bar & Grill and the Sunset Grill. Rejuvenate yourself with a visit to the Summit Spa, or participate in Yoga on the Summit for an experience you will never forget. There is even a full-service video and photography production company available to memorialize your day.

Summertime transforms Sugar Bowl into the perfect venue for weddings, corporate outings, family reunions, and other special events, while the Lodge at Sugar Bowl has exquisite accommodations with gorgeous views. The resort also offers summer dining at Lake Mary and evening dining on Donner Summit. The warm weather brings kids day camps and adult activities as well.

Sugar Bowl is 10 miles west of Truckee, CA, and 45 miles west of Reno on Interstate 80, making it the closest major resort to Sacramento.

There are complimentary hourly shuttles available from Truckee, or the resort can be accessed via the historic gondola or slope-side parking next to the Mt. Judah Day Lodge. The annual snowfall at this resort is 500 inches, so be sure to make good use of the Sugar Bowl web cams when planning your day.

Tahoe Donner Ski Resort
11603 Snowpeak Way. Truckee, CA 96160. (530) 587-9444 Main

Tahoe Donner Ski Resort is a family resort that is committed to instructing the young and the young-at-heart to ski and snowboard. You can count on uncrowded slopes, excellent terrain for beginners, wide-open bowls, and pristine groomed trails. This resort caters to families with interchangeable lift tickets for parents with non-skiing kids, ski lessons for children aged three and up, and even kid-friendly menu items in the cafeteria. The friendly staff is eager to help, providing a personal touch that is often missed at larger resorts.

Tahoe Donner's 120 skiable acres can be explored through 14 groomed runs, and accessed by five lifts. Families will love the tubing and sledding area, where they can enjoy a steaming cup of hot chocolate and other treats when it is time for a break. The Tahoe Donner Cross Country Center will guide skiiers to 51 trails with a combined length of more than 100 kilometers of some of the best cross-country terrain in the area. It has a fully certified cross country ski school to teach useful techniques so you can ski with confidence. All instructors at Tahoe Donner are certified by the Professional Ski Instructors of America and the American Association of Snowboard Instructors.

After a day of playing on the mountain enjoy a delicious meal at the Lodge Restaurant and Pub or head to the Trout Creek Recreation Center. This state-of-the-art fitness facility features a weight room and cardio room, plus an adult lap pool and a recreation pool, steam room, and spas. Fitness classes are available, as well as a massage program and personal trainers. Tahoe Donner is surrounded by a beautiful recreational homeowner community with around 6,500 property owners and more than 30,000 members living in nearby Truckee, CA. It is located 35 miles from Reno, NV, and a mere 5 miles from Donner Lake and 15 miles from Lake Tahoe. Visit Tahoe Donner this season, for a fun and relaxed family vacation.

Ski and Snowboard Rentals

Lake Tahoe is renowned for its world class ski resorts, and North Lake Tahoe ski resorts are in abundance. Start your winter journey at one of the areas excellent ski and snowboard rental shops. Porter Sports is among the best, with three convenient locations filled with the finest in ski and snowboard gear. The professional staff will outfit you with everything you need, from apparel to equipment. Mountain Mikes

Sports is a family owned business offering full service ski and snowboard rentals, plus a demo and tuning shop. Granite Chief in Truckee is a locals favorite carrying great winter and summer gear. Many local shops rent cross country skiing gear as well. If you are looking for an amazing snowboard or skiing adventure, North Lake Tahoe rental shops are ready to serve you!

Granite Chief
11368 Donner Pass Rd. Truckee, CA 96161
Established in 1976, Granite Chief is considered one of the premiere ski and mountain shops at Lake Tahoe and Truckee. You will find their local knowledge of the area ski resorts and backcountry make Granite Chief a valuable resource for locals and visitors alike. The last thirty years Granite Chief has evolved from a one man tuning shop to a full service core ski shop. They now offer full rentals of top of the line skis, demo skis, boots, gear and offer top of the line tuning center. They also sell skis, fit boots, and they have a full lineup of great ski wear for the serious skier.

Mountain Mikes Sports
1602 Squaw Valley Rd. Squaw Valley, CA 96146
Mtn. Mike's Sports has been open since 1988 offering great ski and more recently snowboard rentals. Mtn. Mike's Sports is a family owned, full service ski and snowboard rental, demo and tuning shop. They are proud to offer the latest ski and snowboard equipment at a great price with friendly, quick service. Their ideal location at the base

of Squaw Valley makes for easy pick up and delivery after a day om the slopes.

Porters Sports
100 North Lake Blvd. Tahoe City, CA 96145
Porter Sports is one of North Lake Tahoe's premier ski & snowboard shops with guaranteed customer satisfaction, free shipping, no hassle returns, and price matching. They offer three locations to serve you. Two in Tahoe City and one in historic Truckee, CA. Whether you are looking to rent or own the staff at Porters can get you set up with right skis or snowboard for your level of performance.

Tahoe Bike & Ski
8499 North Lake Blvd. Kings Beach, CA 96143
Tahoe Bike & Ski has been family owned since 1988 offering ski, snowboard, cross country ski, and snowshoe rentals for the whole family. They also provide tune-up services for your ski and snowboard gear. In the summer bring in the family and get your bike rentals for the day. If you are looking for Lake Tahoe souvenirs like T shirts, fleece shirts, sweat shirts, hats, coffee mugs, shot glasses, magnets, pins, patches, post cards, and key chains then pop on in they have it all.

Tahoe Dave's Ski and Boards
590 North Lake Blvd.Tahoe City, CA 96145
Tahoe Dave's Ski and Boards offers five locations including, Kings Beach, Squaw Valley, Truckee and two in Tahoe City. For over 35 years Tahoe Dave's Ski and Boards has been committed to helping you have

a great winter sports experience. Take your pick of their largest selection of rentals and demo equipment on the North Shore. Take an adventure in the backcountry by renting their snowshoes, cross-country gear and rental clothing for the whole family.

The Back Country
11400 Donner Pass Rd # 100. Truckee, CA 96161
The Back Country has two locations to serve you, Truckee and Tahoe City. They offer a wide range of ski and snowboard rental equipment as well as telemark skis and snowshoes. They specialize in high end gear for renting, for sale and also offer back country tours. They also offer a large selection of summer gear for rock climbing, biking, kayaks, canoes and paddleboards.

Village Ski Loft
800 Tahoe Blvd. Incline Village, NV 89451
Located in beautiful Incline Village, Village Ski Loft is the areas best source for quality rental and demo equipment. Every year they add new equipment to their inventory so you can have the best selection of new skis and snowboards to take to the hill. If alpine skiing or snowboarding isn't what you came to Lake Tahoe for, Village Ski Loft provides other winter recreation options like cross country gear, snowshoes, and sleds so you can enjoy the outdoor winter on your own terms.

Sledding, Tubing and Snowparks

Sledding, tubing, snowparks, oh my! What a better way to get the family out enjoying the Lake Tahoe's brisk winter air and fresh new snow then a day at one of the local snowparks. Take pictures of the little ones as they shriek, giggle and laugh on down the hill. Some of the more popular Lake Tahoe tubing parks are Kingvale Tubing And Sledding Center, Northstar Tubing Center, and Squaw Valley's SnoVentures™ Activity Zone. Many areas will charge a fee, but their fun runs and quick access to the top make up for it.

You can also hop in the car and find one of the free parks like Mt. Rose and the West Shore snow play area. Bring your own equipment and don't forget the hot chocolate.

Boreal's Tubing Park at Playland
19749 Boreal Ridge Rd. Soda Springs, CA 95728
Boreal's Playland is a snow tubing park designed for children of all ages the perfect place for family tubing fun. They are equipped with a nicely groomed tubing lanes, easy to use moving carpet, and quality tubes for hours of fun. You will find staff located at the top of the hill to help guide you to the top of the run and look outs at the bottom to help the little ones off the run. You will find Boreal's snow tubing park at Playland at the far end of Boreal's parking lot. There is plenty of good parking and easy walking access to the entrance. Weekends can get busy so plan ahead or try to go mid week. Check out the photo

gallery below for some great pics of the tubing hill, magic carpet and parking. There is a pedestrian charge if you want to view up close.

Located off Hwy. 80 about a 35 minute drive from North Lake Tahoe you will see Boreal ski resort.

Tubing Hours of Operation:
Sunday Thursday 10am 4pm with select Friday, Saturdays & Holidays 10am 8pm
Tubing Session- 2 hr. session $30*

Holiday rates may apply. Only one person per tube and only one person may tube per lane. Personal sleds and personal tubes are not permitted.

Donner Ski Ranch Tubing Hill
Prepare for lots of giggles and laughs as you slide down the snow tubing hill at the Donner Ski Ranch snow park. Once you are at the bottom you can hop on a magic carpet and get whisked to the top again in no time at all. Donner Ski Ranch is located at the top of Donner Summit along historic Route 40.

Granlibakken Ski Area
725 Granlibakken Rd. Tahoe City, CA 96145
Granlibakken Resort features an intimate ski hill, perfect for beginning through intermediate skiers and snowboarders. It's a great place to

avoid the crowds of larger resorts, while enjoying a day of skiing right out your back door.

A rental shop, ski school, warming hut and snack bar are also on the premises. The ski hill, ski school and snack bar are open every Friday through Sunday, every day Christmas/New Years and mid-February holidays. The rental shop, snowplay area and warming hut are open daily all season.

Snowpark: Granlibakken snow park offers an area for saucers only. Rentals available, fee charged for day use

Kingvale Tubing and Sledding Center
Take the Kingvale Exit off Hwy 80. Soda Springs, CA 95728
Kingvale tubing and sledding center offers snow play and sledding for all ages. You will find a snack bar on site to help feed those hungry kids. Bring your own sleds or buy one there for $22. Open Saturday and Sundays and any holidays for snow play and sledding! Parking lot opens at 9:00 am and the snow play begins at 10:00 am. Snow play and sledding $10 per person all day until 4 pm!

Mt. Rose Snow Play Area
Hwy. 431. Incline Village, NV
This hill is located at the top of Mt. Rose highway (Hwy. 431). Located about 8 miles north of Incline Village. Look for a few clearings on the west side of the road. Hills vary in steepness. You must have your own equipment for this large open tubing area. Lots of space and fun to be

had. Drop off your skiers and snow boarders at Mt. Rose Ski Resort and bring the small kids to the snow play area for hours of free fun.

Northstar Tubing Center
5001 Northstar Dr. Truckee, CA 96161

The Northstar Tubing Center offers fun for all ages so get the family on the snow for some heart pumping adventure. The exhilarating ride down the hill will keep the kids happy and busy for hours. Both riders and their tubes are taken by tow lift to the top of the tubing hill where tubers can slide down individually or in daisy chains. The tubing hill itself is J-shaped. You'll cruise down approximately 200 yards and you curve over three whoops that keep you on your toes.

The Northstar Tubing Center is located mid-mountain just above the Northstar Gondola. Get there early since tubing tickets are available on a first-come, first-serve basis only. Get your tickets at the Tickets & Season Pass Office in the Village at Northstar.

Soda Springs Winter Resort
10244 Soda Springs Rd. Soda Springs, CA 96160
Soda Springs says their Tube Town is "The Best Snow Tubing at Tahoe!" Come find out for yourself. Bring the whole family and enjoy the 390° moving carpet is designed to "escalate you up the mountain" in ease and style. Tube Town has expanded their lanes to reduce waiting in line and give you more tubing time. Go skiing and boarding

then take a few turns down the tubing hill since tubing is included with all lift tickets* or can be purchased separately. (*Planet Kids not included) Tube Town at Soda Springs is geared for kids and adults 42" and taller.

Squaw Valley's SnoVentures
1960 Squaw Valley Rd. Squaw Valley, CA 96146
Squaw Valley's SnoVentures™ Activity Zone offers fun for the family. You will find mini snowmobiles for kids ages 6 to 12 where they can ride a snowmobile that is just their size around the mini snowmobile course. Kids must be under 110 pounds and 40" tall. The winter fun continues with tubing at Squaw's three tubing lanes accessed by a covered magic carpet for easy access to the top of the hill. Snow tubes come in two sizes to accommodate adults and kids. Must be ages 3+ and 36" tall.

The SnoVentures™ Lodge is adjacent to the Squaw Valley parking area. Families can warm up in the SnoVentures™ Lodge and enjoy beverages and light food items.

Snowmobiling
Snowmobiling is one of the best ways to experience Lake Tahoe's natural beauty up close. Just imagine speeding past snow crusted pine trees on over 200 miles of maintained trails in Tahoe National Forest. Eagle Ridge Snowmobile Outfitters offers this and so much more. Their thrilling guided snowmobile tours are perfect for beginners and avid

adventurists alike with the highlight being play areas that are exclusive to guests of Eagle Ridge. Lake Tahoe Snowmobile Tours is another great choice. Its spectacular tours lead to North Lake Tahoe's summit where you will experience amazing views of Lake Tahoe and major ski resorts. Designed for all ages and abilities, you won't want to miss an amazing snowmobile mountain adventure. For a different perspective of Lake Tahoe book a South Lake Tahoe snowmobiling tour.

Coldstream Adventures Snowmobile Tours
11760 Donner Pass Rd. Truckee, CA 96161
At Coldstream Adventures Snowmobile Tours you will experience the backcountry magic of winter on their totally private and groomed trails. Coldstream Adventures Snowmobile Tours are located in northern Sierra's Coldstream Canyon west of Truckee California and promises their guided tours will be an exhilarating addition to your visit to Lake Tahoe and Truckee. For the more adventurous type they offer backcountry snowmobile tours with overnight lodging. Since 1995 they have been providing snowmobile tours through beautiful Sierra Mountains.

Eagle Ridge Snowmobile Outfitters
California 89 & Cottonwood Rd Tahoe National Forest, Loyalton, CA 96118. Loyalton, CA 96118
Eagle Ridge Snowmobile Outfitters, Inc. offers memorable guided snowmobile rides through the Tahoe National Forest. Their snowmobile tours cover a wide range of terrain and sites suitable for

all experience levels, from beginner to advanced. At Eagle Ridge Snowmobile Outfitters each trip is personalized to the area your guide will decide so you will experience the most fun and exciting adventure available to your group's abilities. With almost 650 square miles of forest and up to 200 miles of maintained trails, Eagle Ridge Snowmobile Outfitters, Inc. offers the best guided snowmobile rides around.

Lake Tahoe Snowmobile Tours
HWY 267 & Mount Watson Rd. Tahoe Vista, CA 96148
Located in Kings Beach, Lake Tahoe Snowmobile Tours has been providing tours in North Lake Tahoe since 1985. Their tours include spectacular Lake Tahoe views from North Lake Tahoe's summit. Their exciting tours are designed for all ages and ability levels. Lake Tahoe Snowmobile Tours has over 100 miles of trails that travel through the pristine National Forest offering breathtaking views of the Lake Tahoe from Mt. Watson at an elevation of 8200'. Take in the views of some of Lake Tahoe's major ski resorts like Northstar, Squaw Valley, and Alpine Meadows.

Snowmobile Adventures
PO Box 3782. Reno, NV 89505
Sierra Adventures offers snowmobiling adventures like no other, where you effortlessly glide through the high Sierra Mountains taking in the winter wonderland around you. Snowmobiling provides the opportunity to explore various back trails of the Sierra Mountains, as

well as taking you to spectacular views of Lake Tahoe. At Sierra Adventures they provide you the best ride is for your particular skill level and taste. Their guides can take you on wide open, point-to-point runs or on slow moving scenic rides with world-class views. Plan your snowmobile adventure of a lifetime.

Squaw Valley's SnoVentures
1960 Squaw Valley Rd. Squaw Valley, CA 96146
Squaw Valley's SnoVentures™ Activity Zone offers fun for the family. You will find mini snowmobiles for kids ages 6 to 12 where they can ride a snowmobile that is just their size around the mini snowmobile course. Kids must be under 110 pounds and 40" tall. The winter fun continues with tubing at Squaw's three tubing lanes accessed by a covered magic carpet for easy access to the top of the hill. Snow tubes come in two sizes to accommodate adults and kids. Must be ages 3+ and 36" tall.

The SnoVentures™ Lodge is adjacent to the Squaw Valley parking area. Families can warm up in the SnoVentures™ Lodge and enjoy beverages and light food items.

Summer Recreation
North Lake Tahoe Beaches
Lake Tahoe is a vacation hotspot that attracts tourists from all over the world. At 22 miles long and 12 miles wide it is the largest Alpine lake in North America. Visitors are awed by the panoramic mountain views

that can be experienced from every beach on the 72 mile shoreline. August is the warmest month with an average of 78.7 degrees, making it a perfect time to hit the beach!

North Lake Tahoe's Hidden Beach is very popular and located near Incline Village. It's little hard to find and parking is limited, but it is worth the effort to get there. Chimney Beach is a delightful sandy beach that is found six miles south of Incline Village. It is one of Lake Tahoe's dog friendly beaches and attracts a variety of beach-goers. The a little further south is beautiful little D.L. Bliss Beach is a must-stop little piece of paradise that is sheltered in a cove making for a gorgeous setting. It is also popular for camping and hiking.

Looking for a large recreation area? Kings Beach Recreation Area is a great spot for water sport rentals, and attracts families and large groups with its playground, volleyball courts, and shaded picnic tables. Meeks Bay is another recreation area with a fantastic family atmosphere, plus camping, food, boat rentals, and bathrooms with showers. Of course Sand Harbor beach is also at the top of family beaches with it's goreous views, sandy beach and picnic amenities. Hop in the car and head south for some South Lake Tahoe beaches with their special qualities that make them a winner too

Carnelian West Beach
5074 North Lake Boulevard. Carnelian Bay, CA

Carnelian West Beach and Public Lake Access shares the same parking area as North Lake Tahoe's famous Gar Woods Restaurant. Gar Woods maintains Carnelian West Beach on behalf of the California Tahoe Conservancy. This beach stretches 530 feet where you can enjoy benches, picnic tables, BBQ's, restrooms and lovely lakefront promenade. Carnelian West Beach is always open to the public year-round and is considered a pet friendly beach with some limited restrictions to follow.

Carnelian West Beach offers some grassy areas that can be reserved for special events through Gar Woods Restaurant. You will find the shoreline to be pebbly, but still a lovely setting. Spend the day on the beach then take in lunch or dinner on the deck of Gar Woods Restaurant. Of course the Lake Tahoe views are incredible and you will find this public beach to be very clean and easy to access.

Carnelian West Beach is one of many wonderful North Lake Tahoe beaches so come explore the shores of Lake Tahoe up close.

Chambers Landing
6300 Chambers Lodge Road. Homewood, CA 96141
Chambers Landing beach is a small public beach managed by the U.S. Forest Service and located near Homewood, California. Enjoy great views of North Lake Tahoe that will not disappoint. The beach itself is a mixture of sand and some small rocks that gradually descends into

the water making it ideal for little kids. There is a private section of the beach for members of the Beach and Mountain Club.

Spend some time at Chambers Landing Bar and Grill which owns the title of Lake Tahoe's oldest bar. Built over the water Chambers Landing Bar and Grill has become a familiar landmark. They offer a full bar and BBQ menu for those hungry for a good hamburger, grilled chicken sandwich or choice of salads. Chambers Landing beach does not offer any amenities such as BBQ pits or benches. You will find parking along the entrance road which is the only public parking nearby. Plan to get there early to find a parking place and spot on the beach. Dogs are welcome, but required to be on a leash. Chambers Landing is open from sunrise to sunset.

Chimney Beach
Incline Village, NV 89451
Chimney Beach is one of the best ways to get away from the crowds, as long as you're willing to make the moderate half mile hike (one way). Enjoy sweeping views of Lake Tahoe, boulder outcroppings, sandy beach, crystal clear water and the unique chimney marker that gives the beach it's name. There are several sandy beach pockets among boulders as you walk the trail heading south of the Chimney Beach if you want a smaller spot all to yourself. There is a chance you can encounter nude sunbathers so we recommend families staying near the immediate area of Chimney Beach. Picnic tables and

restrooms are provided nearby and feel free to bring your dog since Chimney Beach is a dog friendly Lake Tahoe beach. Get some interesting shots of the chimney which is the only thing remaining of an old lakefront cabin.

The beach is located 2.5 miles south of Sand Harbor right off of Highway 28 (about six miles south of Incline Village, Nevada). There are two parking lots one Forest Service parking lot is .25 miles south of Thunderbird Lodge, on the west side of Highway 28. The second is a more obvious parking lot which is an additional .25 miles south. Parking is free at both parking locations, but overnight camping is not allowed.

There are signs marking the trail near the parking lot restrooms leading you down to the lake. The trail goes straight down from the parking lot and curves back when you get closer to the Lake Tahoe shoreline. You will spot the chimney as you get closer to the beachfront, it's impossible to miss and makes finding this beautiful Lake Tahoe beach a breeze.

Chimney Beach is one of many wonderful North Lake Tahoe beaches. If you are staying in the South Lake Tahoe area then view are guide to South Lake Tahoe beaches too!

Commons Beach
Tahoe City. CA 96145

Commons Beach is the jewel in the heart of Tahoe City. Spanning four acres, it is the site of many community events, such as summertime concerts, movies, music, and a farmer's market. Families love the beachside playground situated among towering trees. It has a structure for the big kids and one for the little tykes, plus an innovative climbing rock. It's the perfect setting for a summer afternoon surrounded by the beautiful view of Lake Tahoe. Come dine in the heart of Tahoe City then take a leisure stroll through Commons Beach and if your in luck catch an early evening summertime concert.

One of Commons Beach best features is the expansive grassy area that the borders the beach, which is a great place for picnicking or a game of catch. Visitors can choose between sunbathing on the soft grass or in the warm sand, and watching the swimmers. Stroll the paved walking/biking path, and rest on the benches in the shade. Picnic sites with barbeques are available, and you can expect bathrooms, free parking, and no animals allowed. Come discover this North Lake Tahoe beach or the many other Lake Tahoe beaches to choose from.

D.L. Bliss State Park, Lester Beach
Lake Tahoe South West Shoreline. CA 96142
Lester Beach and Calawee Cove Beach are located at D.L. Bliss State Park have to be some of Lake Tahoe's most awe inspiring beaches with expansive views of Lake Tahoe. The park location is on the West side of Lake Tahoe, just above Emerald Bay. D.L. Bliss State Park covers

1,830 acres and includes some six miles of magnificent Lake Tahoe shoreline with a popular trail that is worth every step. Although Lester Beach and Calawee Beach are not as expansive as some, they offer more private coves with excellent views. The beach areas are integrated with the camping sites, so visitors claim their piece of the beach early. Beach access can require a little stair navigation in spots, but worth the short treck. Arrive early because the beach parking lot can fill up fast and in case the beach is full check out these other Lake Tahoe beaches that are nearby.

D.L. Bliss State Park Campground
At D.L. Bliss State Park camping is the main draw, with family campsites featuring a table, cupboard and stove, nearby restrooms, and hot showers. There are no hook-ups, but some sites will accommodate 15-foot trailers or 18-foot motorhomes. The group site fits up to 50 people and up to 10 cars. For a little adventure, try one of the 20 primitive campsites that are only accessible by boat. D.L. Bliss State Park campground is on Tahoe's west shore so you might consider it to be a South Lake Tahoe campground or North Lake Tahoe campground the distance there is split.

Boaters can use boat launching facilities about 6 miles of the north or south of the park. Another favorite activity is fishing for Rainbow, Brown and Mackinaw trout, and Kokanee salmon. Lake Tahoe hiking is another draw with many trails to explore, including the Rubicon Point promontory which allows you to see over 100 feet into Lake Tahoe's crystal clear depths. Dogs are allowed in the park, but are not permitted on the trails or beaches. D.L. Bliss State Park is located 14 miles north of South Lake Tahoe, CA and 17 miles south of Tahoe City on Highway 89.

Hidden Beach
South of Incline Village. NV 89451
2018 Update: There is currently road construction and parking in the designated area is no longer available until the work of putting in a new bike path to Sand Harbor is completed. At this time we suggest not visiting this beach. Past Hidden Beach heading south on Hwy. 28 there are other beach options Chimney Beach, Secret Cove and Sand Harbor. Summer months are especially congested and arriving to the beach as early as 9am might be advised in order to get parking within walking/hiking distance to the beaches.

"Hidden in plain sight" might be the best way to describe Lake Tahoe's Hidden Beach. Although it sits right next to Highway 28, you won't even see it unless you stop and peer over the guard rail. The beach itself is flanked by giant boulders with lots of sand for sunbathing, picnicking, and swimming. It's a great place to spend the day just lounging and swimming.

During peak summer months it is recommended you get to the Hidden Beach by 11am for easier parking and optimum choices to spread out your beach gear. Bring plenty of sunscreen, water and even an umbrella if you want some shade. You'll find boaters like to anchor near the waters edge and swim. Also it's common for kayakers and people on stand up paddle board to cruise through. Typically the water near the surface is a bit warmer which makes for a more pleasant dip in the lake.

Unfortunately there is no actual parking lot for Hidden Beach, which means you must park along the highway where permitted and follow a dirt trail on the outside of the guard rail to the beach. The walk is easy going, but not too wide. Many visitors choose to pull over and unload gear and extra passengers right next to the beach and then send the driver off to find parking. Although the parking situation is a little inconvenient, this is what makes Hidden Beach truly secluded. If you want an easier beach to access check out our Lake Tahoe beaches map for other great North Lake Tahoe beaches in the area.

The best parking choices is near the intersection of Lakeshore Boulevard and Hwy. 28 in Incline, Village. Hidden Beach is about a half-mile south of the intersection and you can take the developed trail to the beach. The views and water are amazing so take your camera! This is a wonderful and private place to relax and enjoy Lake Tahoe.

Please note, that Hidden Beach is NOT a clothing optional beach per NRS 201.220. For families we should mention that you might still find a few nude sunbathers on occasion

Hurricane Bay Beach
Tahoe City, CA 96145
Hurricane Bay Beach is located on Lake Tahoe's West Shore where local homeowners moor their boats in this beautiful bay. It's easy to spot and parking made simple since the road skirts along the shoreline with parking spots right off the main road. This makes this beach an ideal "quick stop" to take a dip in the lake, exercise your dog, enjoy the sunset or picnic without having to haul all your beach items to far to the shore.

Hurricane Bay Beach extends across a half mile of shoreline with great North Lake Tahoe views and amazing crystal clear water. We recommend bringing chairs since the beach consists of smooth small rocks and not the decomposed granite found at other Lake Tahoe beaches. Hurricane Bay Beach is one of Lake Tahoe's dog friendly beaches with a 50 foot designated "dog friendly" section. Enjoy the paved bike/walking path that runs along the beach and heads north into Tahoe City. There are public restrooms and picnic tables at the south end of the beach along the paved bike path

Incline Beach & Private Incline Beaches

967 Lakeshore Blvd, Incline Village, NV 89451
Come enjoy Incline Beach, Ski Beach, and Burnt Cedar Beach & Pool you will need a valid Beach Access IVGID Recreation Pass, daily beach pass or a Recreation Punch Card available at the Parks & Recreation Department located at the Incline Village Recreation Center (980 Incline Way). These passes are for local property owners and their family members.

If you cruise down Lakeshore Drive you will see these three beaches located between the Hyatt Regency and Hwy 28. These beaches are beautiful and set up for family fun, but require a pass to get in. If you don't have a pass we recommend you head to other nearby public beaches like <u>Kings Beach State Park Beach</u> or <u>Sand Harbor</u>.

Incline Beach
967 Lakeshore Blvd., Incline Village, NV 89451
At Incline Beach you have access to a snack bar, designated swim area, picnic tables and grills, kids playground and of course a sandy beach to soak in the Tahoe sunshine.

Ski Beach
967 Lakeshore Blvd., Incline Village, NV 89451
At Ski Beach you can launch your boat, enjoy established picnic areas, a volleyball and bocce ball court.
Gate hours are 8:00 am 6:00 pm daily during the season.

Burnt Cedar Beach & Pool

665 Lakeshore Blvd., Incline Village, NV 89451

Burnt Cedar Beach & Pool is known for it's heated pool, and more intimate beach setting with picnic areas with grills, snack bar, kids playground and a more private sandy beach.

Kings Beach State Park and Boat Launch

8318 N. Lake Blvd., Hwy. 28. Kings Beach, CA 96143

Welcome to Kings Beach, the largest public beach on the North Shore! Explore its nearly 700 feet of shoreline or spend the day on the water with a rental from North Tahoe Watersports. Rent a Jet Ski, kayak, water bike, or paddle boat, or enjoy a parasailing ride or private lake tour. Swimmers claim Kings Beach has one of the warmest beaches on Lake Tahoe do to the fact that it is south-facing and has a gradually deepening lake floor. There is a parking fee, but walkers and bikers can use the beach at no charge. Kings Beach also has the only public dog friendly beach on the North Shore so bring your pooch and your doggy bags.

Enjoy a stroll on the walking paths that meander throughout King Beach Plaza and its patio-style courtyard. It is the site of many special events, including the summertime arts and crafts fairs. This beach is dialed with bathrooms, a basketball court, volleyball courts, horseshoes, barbeque and picnic areas, and a lakefront playground. The recreation area is in downtown Kings Beach, just off of Highway 28.

Coon Street Boat Launch

Boaters can head to the Coon Street Boat Launch, which has restrooms and parking for vehicles with or without trailers. Expect separate fees for launching and parking, which is limited. Coon Street Boat Launch is located at the south end of Kings Beach State Park with easy access to North Lake Tahoe. Check out other nearby Lake Tahoe boat launches.

Hours for Coon Street Boat Launch: 7:00 AM 7:00 PM, Thursday Monday (Closed Tuesday and Wednesday)

Meeks Bay Resort and Marina

7941 Emerald Bay Rd. Meeks Bay, CA 96142
Families love Meeks Bay for its spacious white sandy beach and lakeside picnic areas. The large designated swimming area is accessed easily from the parking lot (which requires a fee). For your convenience there is an onsite food stand, bathrooms, and a full-service retail store where you will find a full assortment of Native American crafts, books, clothing and apparel. Designated barbeque areas can be reserved for small and large groups. The boat dock, snack bar and general store are all handicap accessible. During the peak summer months be sure to get there early to find your perfect spot. The beach is busier then most, but the amenities and easy access make it a winner. If you get there late and the beach parking is full then check out other nearby North Lake Tahoe beaches.

The full-service marina offers rentals of canoes, paddle boats and kayaks, and provides Lake Tahoe boat tours and fishing excursions. Fishermen try to catch Mackinaw trout from the shore or on a full-service charter. Some visitors use Meeks Bay as the trailhead to Desolation Wilderness.

Do you want to stay for more than a day? Accommodations at Meeks Bay range from cozy log cabins and lakefront lodging, to the Washoe House and the historic Kehlet Mansion. Unfortunately, pets are not allowed anywhere in the resort. Visit Meeks Bay — just 25 miles south of Truckee, CA, and 16 miles north of South Lake Tahoe, CA.

North Lake Tahoe Beach
7860 North Lake Blvd. Kings Beach, CA 96143
Families, couples, and individuals alike love North Lake Tahoe Beach. It is a quaint 2.7 acres with 540 feet of shoreline, making it a little less crowded than some of the larger beaches. Kick off your shoes and enjoy a game of sand volley ball in one of the three beachside courts, or toss some horseshoes in the horseshoe pit. The picnic area is wheelchair accessible with paved walkways, plus barbeque grills, benches, and picnic tables.

Parties of up to 90 people will love the group shelter with its large barbeque, running water and picnic tables. Call ahead and rent for it for a beachside wedding, party, or reunion. When not reserved, it is available on a first-come-first-serve basis. It has a seasonal visitor information booth, restrooms, and free parking. North Lake Tahoe Beach is located at the intersection of Highway 28 and Highway 267.

Sand Harbor
Incline Village. NV 89451
Sand Harbor is located along State Route 28, just three miles south of Incline Village. The area offers 55 acres of paradise expansive sandy beaches, rocky coves, and panoramic views of the east shoreline. Swimmers and scuba divers enjoy the interesting rock formations, gently sloping beaches, and Lake Tahoe's trademark crystal clear water. Boaters and beach goers alike will want to get an early start in the summer, because the boat launch fills up fast! It includes two wave protected double ramps with docks and adjacent parking.

During the summer months Sand Harbor features a visitor center and gift shop, snack bar and grill, and group area for up to 100 guests. Pets are not allowed and you can also expect a parking fee, bathrooms, watercraft inspections, and Beach Patrol in the summer months. Once you get there you will soon discover why this is one of Lake Tahoe's best beaches. You don't have to limit yourself to Sand Harbor when there many other great North Lake Tahoe beaches nearby.

Families love the shaded picnic areas with tables and barbeques. The paved walkways make them wheel chair accessible and the Sand

Harbor Nature Trail is also handicap-accessible. It is 1/3 mile long and offers interpretive signs and gorgeous views. There is also a ½ mile trail to Memorial Point, with access to secluded beaches and rock areas to explore. Come in July and August for the popular Lake Tahoe Shakespeare Festival. It's a "most attend" event if your vacationing in the summer.

Keep Sand Harbor safe and clean by observing the following:

No bottles are allowed in waterfront areas

Fires permitted in designated areas only

No pets are allowed

Stay on trails

No camping is allowed at Hwy. 28 beaches

Leave no trace

Plants, animals, rocks, minerals and artifacts are protected by state law

Litter must be properly disposed.

Secret Cove Beach
Lake Tahoe East Shore.Incline Village, NV 89451
Secret Cove Beach on Lake Tahoe's east shore is located along Highway 28 not too far from other popular Lake Tahoe beaches like Chimney Beach and Sand Harbor. Secret Cove is one of those signature Lake Tahoe photo spots and you can see why. This gorgeous little cove is surrounded by granite boulders, sandy shoreline and the crystal

clear water is just captivating. On any given summer weekend you will find a group of devoted regulars who pack in their colorful umbrellas, beach chairs and come to soak in the sun most of them in the nude. This is one of Lake Tahoe's nude beaches and if you wear a bathing suit you might be in the minority. Many regulars take pride in keeping the Secret Cove Beach clean, fun and friendly. Get there early to claim your spot especially when the Lake Tahoe water level is high and sandy spots become limited. Secret Cove is a Lake Tahoe dog friendly beach with restrictions respect others, use your leash and pack out all dog waste.

Secret Cove Beach is located about 2.6 miles south of Sand Harbor right off of Highway 28 (about six miles south of Incline Village, Nevada). Parking can be a challenge especially during peak summer season so arrive early to get a spot in the only designated parking lots. There are two parking lots one on the lake side and another across the road a bit further down. Parking is free at both parking locations, but overnight camping is not allowed. If these lots are full then you can also park along the lake side of the road further south on Hwy 28 just past the "no parking" signs. From the road you will see designated trails built by the U.S. Forrest Service that lead down to the lake, but keep in mind they can be fairly steep. Signs have been posted a long parts of the trail to guide you to your destination. If you were lucky enough to park in the lake side parking lot then start your journey at the gate. The fire access road beyond the gate will take you down to the trail that peals off to the right and down to Secret Cove. There are bathrooms provided along the trail and trash bins. Please pack out what you pack in and don't forget to use sunblock. The higher altitude can burn your skin quickly if you are not prepared.

Skunk Harbor
North East, Lake Tahoe. NV 89451
Skunk Harbor is one of North Lake Tahoe's hidden beaches. It can only be accessed by hiking or biking the 1.6-mile long trail. The "trail" is actually an old road with a lot of history. As you hike, see if you can spot the remains of an old railroad grade, which was built in the 1870s to supply timber to Virginia City. The road winds through a mixed conifer forest with wonderful Lake Tahoe views and eventually splits off in two directions. The left fork leads to Prey Meadows where you can picnic next to a creek among fragrant wildflowers. The right fork will take you to the picturesque cove and Skunk Harbor beach which tends to be less crowded, yet still stunning as you can see from the photos.

The cove is a favorite destination for sunbathers and swimmers in the summer. The cove even features a large gray stone building that was built in the 1920s by a prominent family from San Francisco who used it as a secluded picnic spot. The Skunk Harbor hiking trail is good for kids and dogs, and can even handle a beefy stroller. The trail down is fairly easy and quick, but sure to plan for the hike out since it can be a bit of a climb for the little ones. Good shoes recommended even though the decomposed granite trail is fairly smooth. The trail is open from March to November and dogs are allowed off the leash.

Skunk Harbor is located on Highway 28 about two miles north of Highway 50. Parking is limited to the turnouts along the road, and the trail head is marked by a green pipe gate on the west side of the highway. There is no parking fee, just make sure you don't park in front of the gate or you might get fined. If you don't mind a little hiking, this is definitely a must-see beach.

Sugar Pine Point State Park
Just south of Tahoma. Tahoma, CA 96142
Bordering Lake Tahoe for almost two miles, Sugar Pine Point State Park is the largest state park at Lake Tahoe. Explore its 2,000 acres filled with sugar pine, aspen, juniper, and fir forests, plus 3.5 miles that extends into the Desolation Wilderness Area. Discover beachfront trails, gorgeous hikes, campground, swimming holes, and boating opportunities. Reconnect with the past at the <u>Hellman-Ehrman Mansion</u>, an early 1900s summer retreat. Take the challenge of fishing for Mackinaw, Kokanee Salmon, and Rainbow Trout.

Location, Fees, and Operating Hours

Sugar Pine Point State Park can be found on the west shore of Lake Tahoe just 10 miles south of Tahoe City, CA, on Highway 89.

The Day Use Annual Pass is accepted here, and you can expect day-use parking fees to start around $8. For camping fees and park hours call the park office at (530) 525-7982.

The <u>Hellman-Ehrman Mansion</u> is open from Memorial Day weekend through Labor Day. For current tour times and ticket prices call (530) 525-7232.

Activities and Adventures

Sugar Pine Point State Park is meant to be explored and discovered! You can grab a map and head out on your own, or take advantage of guide services and programs.

Start your summer adventure at the Nature Center and Gift Shop, located in the Tank House and open daily from June to the end of August, plus weekends in September. Immerse yourself in the region's geology and natural history with hands-on exhibits, interpretive displays, and an educational theater. This is also the place to get recreational guides and books.

Walk on the <u>Dolder Nature Trail</u>, which circles the Edwin L. Z'berg Natural Preserve and other <u>easy nature trails</u>. Check out the Junior Ranger Program for children between the ages 7 to 12. This summer program is led by the park staff and offers wonderful activities that foster an appreciation of our cultural and natural heritage. The park has many Hiking and Nature Trails that can be explored on your own with an informative brochure, or with a live guide in the spring, summer, and fall when staff is available. Overnight adventurists head to the General Creek Campground with its 175 sites that are open year-round.

Summer Fun!

Sugar Pine State Park's beachfront encompasses 7,000 feet. Enjoy swimming and fishing at the pier. Gently sloping lawns shaded by towering trees provide the perfect lakeside picnic spot. Bicyclists love to ride the West Shore Bike Trail. Play a game of tennis on the Hellman-Ehrman Mansion's tennis court, or tour the Pine Lodge's two boathouses to see the boats that helped start Lake Tahoe boating events. Boaters can launch, moor, and rent boats at nearby marinas, such as Obexer's Boat Company, located in Homewood. Unfortunately, boats cannot be beached or moored overnight at Sugar Pine Point State Park due to space limitations. Within just a few miles drive are other great Lake Tahoe beaches you might want to check out while visiting the area.

Love camping? Then book your next campsite at General Creek Campground, one of the largest in the Lake Tahoe basin. The scenic forest setting, paved roads, bike path, hiking trails and campground amenities make this an ideal Lake Tahoe campground.

Snow Activities

Wintertime brings a whole different kind of exploration with Guided Cross Country Ski/Snowshoe Excursions. Beginner and intermediate cross country skiers enjoy the easy terrain at Sugar Pine Point State Park. With 18.7 kilometers to explore, you will discover five color-coded trails that range from one to three miles in length. Sugar Pine is rich in Olympic history. Yes, you heard it right, the VIII Winter Olympics were held here in 1960. Check out the General Creek Trail, which takes you to the center of where the men's events took place. The biathlon as well as the men's cross country events were held here.

Activity schedules and interpretive guides are available online or by calling the park office (530) 525-7982 (snow phone), (530) 525-7232 (information). The two groomed cross-country ski trails can be explored on your own as well, and ski and snowshoe lessons are available on many weekends during the winter. This park is not dog friendly.

General Creek Campground is also the only site for winter camping on Lake Tahoe. There several other great cross country skiing trails and downhill ski resorts in the Lake Tahoe basin to keep you busy this winter.

Tahoe Vista Recreation Area and Boat Launch

7010 North Lake Blvd. Tahoe Vista, CA 96148

Tahoe Vista Recreation Area and Boat Launch underwent a total reconstruction that was completed in the summer 2006. Come enjoy the beach and picnic area on the 2.7 acre lakeshore property, with approximately 800 feet of lakeshore frontage. The Recreation Area includes lake access, a sheltered boat launching facility, picnic area, restrooms, sidewalks, and a large plaza area with interpretive signage. This is a Tahoe Vista local's favorite so come get out on Lake Tahoe or catch some rays on the beach. One of North Lake Tahoe's more quaint beaches to discover and the boat launch is easy to navigate.

Hours for Tahoe Vista Recreation Area: 7:00 AM 8:00 PM, 7 Days a week

North Lake Tahoe Bike Rentals

Your summertime mountain bike adventure awaits! Coast along the beautiful and scenic Truckee River, catch some speed at the bike parks at Northstar or Squaw Valley USA, or get a little more extreme on the Emigrant Trail or Tahoe Rim. Whether you are a beginner or advanced, Northstar at Tahoe Bike Park will hook you up with equipment rentals, chair lift access, and over 2,000 acres of bike trails with amazing views. Visit the professionals at Cyclepaths Mountain Bike, conveniently located on Lake Tahoe's west shore bike path where the staff can equip you and then point you to the best biking trails in the area.

Cyclepaths Mountain Bike
10200 Donner Pass Rd. Truckee, CA 96161
Cycle Paths is located in downtown historic Truckee, the gateway to the Sierra Mountains. Come rent or test drive your dream bike today Road, XC, All Mountain , DH, Cruiser, Hybrid, Kids Bikes. They have knowledge of the most popular biking trails in the area. Cruise along the scenic Truckee River on the Legacy Trail, tear up the bike park at Northstar or Squaw, take off on a full suspension bike to Emigrant Trail or hop a shuttle to the Tahoe Rim. Come in and they will hook you up.

Factory Biking
3039 River Rd. Squaw Valley, CA 96146
Corner of Hwy 89 and Squaw Valley Rd. North Lake Tahoe's beautiful bike trail system offers a fun and healthy way to access Lake Tahoe and the Truckee River. Factory Biking's convenient location at the beginning of the bike trail has plenty of easy parking. They offer a variety of stylish, comfortable cruisers

Northstar Mountain Bike Park
5001 Northstar Drive. Truckee, CA 96161
Northstar Mountain Bike Park center has everything you need for an exciting summer mountain and road biking adventures. They offer everything from beginner to advanced cross country and downhill mountain biking trails, lift-access, bike rentals and bike shop services. Vacationers and locals come together for fun Thursday night country bike races at Northstar. Trail system, accessed via chair lifts (2000 acres). Bike rentals available.

Northstar Bike Accademy offers a variety of group, private lessons, clinics as well as camps throughout the season to help bring you to the next level.

Olympic Bike Shop
620 North Lake Blvd. Tahoe City, CA 96145
Olympic Bike Shop is one of North Lake Tahoe's premiere bike shop for rentals, sales, and service. For over 30 years the Olympic Bike Shop has been the epicenter of cycling activity for the Tahoe Truckee Region. Nearby bike trails are easily accessible from Olympic Bike Shop such as Truckee River path, West Shore path, and Dollar Hill path. Olympic Bike Shop carefully selects bikes that have proven reputations of performance and durability.

Tahoe Bike & Ski
8499 North Lake Blvd. Kings Beach, CA 96143
Tahoe Bike & Ski has been family owned since 1988 offering ski, snowboard, cross country ski, and snowshoe rentals for the whole family. They also provide tune-up services for your ski and snowboard gear. In the summer bring in the family and get your bike rentals for the day. If you are looking for Lake Tahoe souvenirs like T shirts, fleece shirts, sweat shirts, hats, coffee mugs, shot glasses, magnets, pins, patches, post cards, and keychains then pop on in they have it all.

North Lake Tahoe Bike Trails

Lake Tahoe biking trails offer breathtaking scenery and an adrenaline rush like you have never experienced before! Beginners can enjoy easy cross country trail rides, while advanced riders get a thrill out of technical downhill runs. The Flume Trail mountain bike trail is outstanding with easy to moderate terrain and incredible views. The ride up to Watson Lake is fairly secluded and offers a great workout. If you are looking for bike rentals and services, check out Northstar Mountain Bike Park Center, which is also a great resource for excellent North Lake Tahoe bike trails. Quench your thirst for adventure by exploring some of the many Lake Tahoe biking trails!

Brockway Summit to Watson Lake
Watson Lake Rd. (Park top of Broakway Summit). CA

Distance: 13.4 miles round trip
Elevation Change: 7000 ft. to 7760 ft.

Hiking Watson Lake Trail:
Casual hikers love Watson Lake for it's beauty and seclusion. It is a perfect site for a picnic and swim with gorgeous views, wildflowers, and small wildlife. The trail is more of a scenic path on fairly flat terrain for the first 4.5 miles then a gentle climb for 2.2 miles to Watson Lake. A small area of the path can be a bit soupy until it dries out in the later part of summer. On the trail you will come across forest service roads, specifically Fiberboard Freeway (FSR 73) and the

Tahoe Rim Trail meets up with the road in several locations. The hike is not ideal for young kids because of the length of the hiking trail. You can drive into the lake if you prefer and enjoy other trail offshoots along the way.

Optional Biking Route—Mt Watson Road to Watson Lake:

Bikers enjoy riding up the road that leads to Watson Lake. This a moderate to difficult trail for most riders. The road is fairly isolated, smooth trail making it a fun ride to the lake. Expect some moderately difficult climbing with some fast descents, and one steady 2.2 mile climb that will give you a good workout. You will pass over several streams before reaching the lake. Relax and unwind before heading back or you can continue on the main Mt. Watson road which continues on toward Tahoe City and eventually turns into a dirt road.

Directions: To get to Watson Lake from Downtown Truckee, CA, head east onto Brockway Road, and turn right onto Brockway Road (Highway 276)—this will take you up Brockway Grade. Brockway trailhead is on about 0.5 miles south of Brockway Summit. Park and start your journey to Watson Lake.

Emigrant Trail
Hwy 89 (Start at Donner Picnic Area). Truckee, CA 96141
This is Truckee's most popular mountain biking trail, but is also a great hiking trail worth exploring. Truckee's Emigrant Trail offers stunning

scenery, mellow rolling single-track, the perfect early-season biking warm-up what's not to love about the Emigrant Trail? Beginner and intermediate riders alike can hit this trail in early spring as it is one of the first trails to lose its winter snow. Families adore this trail, groups with differing skill levels find it a great compromise, and beginners find it a boost to their skills and confidence.

Most rider (or hikers!) start at the Donner Party Camp Picnic Area parking lot and the image gallery showcases this starting point. Right from the start the trail runs parallel to the north side of Prosser Creek. After you leave the creek, expect to cross a number of dirt roads. Don't worry; the main crossings are well marked and the minor crossings are obvious. Enjoy rolling hills on this out-and-back adventure, with very few minor technical spots. The uphill runs are minimal, but you can still enjoy some fast sections through open valleys. Enjoy swimming in the Stampede Reservoir to cool off in the summer months. In May and June enjoy beautiful wildflowers while the mountain scenery is guaranteed to be stunning year-round.

Starting from Downtown Truckee, heading northeast on Donner Pass Rd., you will come to the roundabout where you merge onto SR 89N. Continue about 4.5 miles to the Donner Camp picnic area located on the right.

Emigrant Trail is popular on the weekends and at the peak of the tourist season, making it a little crowded the first mile or two. Total riding time is just over 2 hours. In the early spring the trail can be a bit muddy in parts. If you are looking to gain a deep love of mountain biking, ride this trail once and you will be hooked.

Flume Trail Mountain Bike Trail
3709 Hwy 28 (Start at Spooner Lake). Glenbrook, NV 89413
For an easy to moderate mountain biking experience, hit the Flume Trail on the east side of Lake Tahoe. This 14-mile long trail follows a mountain ridge overlooking Spooner Lake, best known for its incredible views and cliff-hugging sections of trail. It is one of the most popular Lake Tahoe mountain biking trails and once you experience it you will understand why. Overall it is an easy ride on mostly dirt roads with some sandy trail conditions and a technical single-track section that covers from Marlette Lake to the Tahoe Rim Trail junction.

Start at the Spooner Lake day-use area (parking fee required), just look for the signs to the trailhead. You can expect some hairpin turns and a steep 4-mile climb that gets a little sandy at the end, which some bikers find to be the most challenging aspect of the trail. It ends with a 0.8-mile downhill trek to Marlette Lake. Marlette Lake is a great place to take a break, swim or catch a bite to eat before continuing on. After arriving at Marlette Lake, you will follow a dirt road around the west side of the lake for about 1.6 miles to the Flume Trailhead. The fun starts here with 4.5 miles of rolling, slightly downhill track. Take in the amazing Flume Trail views from 1600' above the east shore of Lake Tahoe. Once you reach the "Y" you can go left where the trail decends 1600' to Highway 28 where you can pay a fee to take the shuttle back, or go right to continue on the Flume Trail, following the loop back to the park which will add another 1.5 to 3 hours on to your trip.

On the Flume Trail, your mountain biking skills don't have to be too technical, but expect to get a great cardio workout. Just make sure you are comfortable using braking techniques and smooth turns in sand, and expect to be on the trail for 1.5 to 3 hours. More seasoned riders can expect to complete the trail in roughly an hour (going one way). The start of the Flume Trail at Spooner Lake is not far from the California-Nevada state line and South Lake Tahoe casinos.

Glenshire Lake
Glenshire Clubhouse. Truckee, CA 96161
Nestled among alpine peaks of Truckee, the Glenshire Lake loop is relaxing and simple to navigate, making it perfect for families with young children. This area has lots of gently rolling hills and gorgeous mountain views. Part of the scenic trail crosses a lush meadow of wildflowers as it circles around the quaint lake on gentle terrain. Take an evening stroll in the soft glow of a gorgeous sunset, or enjoy your walk under the twinkling stars. Dogs on a leash are welcome. For

something more challenging visit the North Lake Tahoe hiking trails directory.

Directions: To get to the trailhead from downtown Truckee go east on Donner Pass Road, take a right on Glenshire Drive and drive 5 miles to the Glenshire Clubhouse parking lot (on the left). The trailhead is behind the clubhouse.

Bikers Please Note: Glenshire Drive is not biker friendly due to a lack of shoulders and high speeds.

Northstar Mountain Bike Park
5001 Northstar Drive. Truckee, CA 96161
Northstar Mountain Bike Park center has everything you need for an exciting summer mountain and road biking adventures. They offer everything from beginner to advanced cross country and downhill mountain biking trails, lift-access, bike rentals and bike shop services. Vacationers and locals come together for fun Thursday night country bike races at Northstar. Trail system, accessed via chair lifts (2000 acres). Bike rentals available.

Northstar Bike Accademy offers a variety of group, private lessons, clinics as well as camps throughout the season to help bring you to the next level.

Sawtooth Trail

Off US Forest Service 06. Truckee, CA 96160

This adventure takes mountain bikers, runners, and day-hikers along the ridge between Squaw Valley and Northstar ski resorts. Many Truckee local's like to bike the Sawtooth Trail for a fun excursion that is not too difficult. The gentle rolling single-track trail snakes through some rocky, sparse forest areas. The elevation gain tops off at 500 feet, and while most of the track is smooth dirt there is a challenging section with a lot of scree deposits. It is recommended that you take the trail counterclockwise, so that you descend on this loose rock area instead of climbing up through it. Points of interest along the trail include two overlooks into the Truckee River Canyon that offer gorgeous views of the Truckee River. This trail also connects with other routes on the Mt. Watson network of trails if you choose to make this a more difficult or extended mountain bike ride. Check other North Lake Tahoe biking and hiking trails nearby like the Watson Lake trail.

Directions: The Sawtooth Trail is located in the South part of Truckee, CA, along Highway 89 that heads south of Lake Tahoe. To get there from the center of Truckee, head east on Brockway Road (Highway 267) going towards Northstar Resort, turn right on Palisades Drive, then turn right on Silver Fir, and then left on Thelin Road. Turn right on US Forest Service 06 and drive about ½ mile to the Sawtooth trailhead (on the right). Old forest service roads intersect the trail many times, but if you stick to the single-track it is easy remain on course.

Tahoe XC, Tahoe City

925 Country Club Drive. Tahoe City, CA 96145

Discover serene meadow trails, challenging hills, and a few thrilling downhill areas at Tahoe XC in Tahoe City. The setting is ideal for cross country skiers and snowshoeing enthusiasts of all abilities. Its 22 trails, spanning more than 65 km, sport stunning Lake Tahoe views. Nine kilometers of trails are machine groomed daily. Three warming huts offer free hot chocolate and pose as resting spots along the trails.

Tahoe XC is one of the few places in North Lake Tahoe that has dog-friendly trails. The two trails open to dogs and are groomed daily and cover 9 km. They offer PSIA certified instruction, plus rentals for skate, classic, and snowshoe, pull-behind sleds for kids (55 pounds or less), and kids gear. Grab a bite to eat at the Day Lodge Café and enjoy free WiFi. Tahoe XC is host to the start of the Great Ski Race, one of the largest cross country ski events in the western United States, and is located only three miles from the convenience of downtown Tahoe City.

Summer at Tahoe XC

Come in the summer when Tahoe Cross Country in Tahoe City offers trailhead mountain biking as well as bike rentals and more. Enjoy their convenient trailhead mountain bike rentals, food service, retail and repair shop. Tahoe Cross Country offers fantastic trails for beginner and intermediate riders, and there is also easy access to advanced terrain higher up. There is great terrain for all ages and abilities, riding or hiking.

Boating and Watersports

Throw on your suit and lather that sunscreen because your vacation isn't complete until you've experienced some North Lake Tahoe boating and watersports. Take in the views as you skirt along the shoreline looking for the perfect beach or hidden cove. Whether you book a Lake Tahoe boat rental, jet ski, kayak or canoe there are many great North Lake Tahoe businesses ready to give you a great vacation experience.

Walk in the doors of North Tahoe Watersports, Inc.and let the fun begin! They offer parasailing, private lake tours, personal watercraft rentals and human-powered boating options. Tahoe Water Adventures is another excellent choice for watercraft rentals, plus professional water ski lessons and beautiful scenic boat tours. High Sierra Water Ski School has excellent waterski and wakeboard instructors, plus an extensive line of rental equipment.

Imagine soaring above the lake on a thrilling Lake Tahoe parasailing excursion, or relaxing on a private lake tour. Lake Tahoe jet ski rentals allow you to choose your own adventure and schedule. No matter how you decide to get on pristine waters of Lake Tahoe, the opportunity to be surrounded by the most fantastic views in the world will be the climax of your Tahoe vacation

Action Watersports

Three Locations at Lake Tahoe. CA 96150
Action Watersports of Lake Tahoe has three locations on the lake offering Lake Tahoe boating options. Camp Richardson Marina and Lakeside Marina locations are in South Lake Tahoe and the third location is at Meeks Bay Marina on the West Shore. Action Watersports will get you on Lake Tahoe for some fun and excitement. They offer some of the best selection of water sport rentals kayaks, paddleboats, jet skis, waverunners, water skis and Four Winn power boats. Book an exhilarating afternoon of parasailing from their state-of-the-art boat and get a new perspective of Lake Tahoe high above the water. For the ultimate in adrenaline rush ride on Lake Tahoe book the Tahoe Thunder, California's fastest Coast Guard-certified speedboat ride. Kids and adults alike will smile with joy as they speed along the surface of Lake Tahoe.

High Sierra Water Ski School

1850 West Lake Blvd. Tahoe City, CA 96145
High Sierra Water Ski School offers two convenient locations to serve you one at the Sunnyside Restaurant, Lodge & Marina and the second on the West Shore at the Homewood High & Dry Marina. They offer water skiing and wakeboard lessons, boat rentals, boat charters, jet ski

rentals, along with canoe, kayak and equipment rentals. High Sierra Water Ski School invites you to experience Lake Tahoe's most fun and exciting summer recreation operation, perfect for family boat trips and summer vacation activities.

North Tahoe Watersports, Inc.
8398 N. Lake Blvd. Kings Beach, CA 96143
North Tahoe Watersports, Inc. has two locations on the North Shore of Lake Tahoe where you will find they are your one stop for watersports excitement and fun. They offering parasailing, private lake yours, personal watercraft rentals and a complete line of non motorized rentals such as kayaks and canoes. Their Tahoe City location at Tahoe City Marina is for their parasailing only. The Kings Beach location is for all your other water fun rentals.

SUP to You Tahoe
Rim Drive. Tahoe Vista, CA 96148
SUP to You Tahoe is a mobile, North Lake Tahoe based stand up paddle board rental company. We differ from other paddle board rental businesses because we bring the fun to you. Why drive around all day looking for a place to rent paddle boards when you could be heading to your favorite beach with them in your car? Reserve a rental ahead of time, and we'll drop the board(s) off at a location of your choosing. We'll happily deliver rental almost anywhere in North Lake Tahoe!

SWA's North Lake Tahoe Boat Rentals

569 McDonald Dr. Incline Village, NV 89451
SWA's North Lake Tahoe Boat Rentals offering Lake Tahoe boat rentals and VIP boat service. When renting one of our premium Lake Tahoe rental boats we'll make sure your rental experience is a safe and memorable one. There is no better way to relax while soaking up Tahoe's shear beauty from the water's perspective. We guarantee a well maintained, clean and dependable vessel equipped with all required USCG approved safety equipment. Our Tahoe boat rentals range from 20' 28' with capacities of up to 11 people. Fuel is included in our prices (no hidden fees here). Your rental boat will come fully fueled to make your experience that much more worry free and enjoyable!

Tahoe City Marina and Mall
700 North Lake Blvd. Tahoe City, CA 96145

The Marina is one of the oldest Lake Tahoe marinas and is full service marina offering a full line of boating and recreational fun. You will find several recreational outfitters including daily parasailing, sailing cruises, kayak rentals and various fishing charter boats. Marina services include boat rentals, slip and buoy rentals, indoor winter boat storage, forklift and travelift, launching (no public ramp) and fuel sales. Located in a historic building that is headquarters to the Tahoe Yacht Club which host the annual Lake Tahoe wooden boat show "Concours d'Elegance."

- ✓ Boat launch (no public ramp)
- ✓ Fuel dock with regular fuel
- ✓ Docks, slips, and moorings
- ✓ Pump out station
- ✓ Restaurant and shopping
- ✓ Restrooms
- ✓ Repair facility nearby
- ✓ Boat sales, rentals and storage

Tahoe City Marine Supply
700 North Lake Blvd. Tahoe City, CA 96145
Tahoe City Marine Supply offers all your Lake Tahoe boating supplies including wakeboards, wakesurfs, boating accessories and more. They offer a large selection of wakeboard rentals, wakesurf rentals, tube rentals, water ski rentals, wetsuit rentals, and life jacket rentals. Check out our rental rates.

Need new summer swimw wear? Then drop in and check out their latest bathing suits, board shorts, flip flops, and sunscreen. Tahoe City Marine Supply sells everything you will need to make the most out of your next boat trip and keep you lookin stylish on the lake. They carry the latest from REEF, O'Neill, Liquid Force, and our own awesome custom gear!

Tahoe Eco-Sports

8612 North Lake Blvd. Kings Beach, CA 96143

Since 1991 Tahoe Eco-Sports has been the one stop adventure shop for locals and visitors looking to experience Lake Tahoe's North Shore up close and personal. They are a full service paddle sports shop with kayak rentals, stand up paddleboard rentals, sailboat rentals and accessories. Tahoe Eco-Sports offers a variety of Lake Tahoe guided kayak tours, even a full moon tour! They are the only Tahoe company offering year-round guided kayak tours on the lake and provide winter dry suits for safety and comfort. You will find them located next to the Kings Beach boat ramp on Coon St. and Hwy. 28. Once you are in the water you're just minutes from the wonderful, giant boulders in Crystal Bay.

Tahoe Paddle & Oar

8299 N Lake Blvd. Kings Beach, CA 96143

Tahoe Paddle & Oar is located in beautiful Kings Beach on the North Shore of Lake Tahoe. They offer top-end canoes, kayaks and paddleboard rentals as well as instruction, guided kayak tours and a full service paddlesport retail store. Their most popular tour is into Crystal Bay, which features natural hot springs and gigantic boulder mazes. Tahoe Paddle & Oar offers team building activities for small groups and your larger, corporate events.

Tahoe Water Adventures

120 Grove St. Tahoe City, CA 96145. Tahoe City, CA 96145
Let Tahoe Water Adventures handle all of your watercraft needs this summer at North Lake Tahoe. They offer hourly to multi-day rentals of their inventory of boats, "JetSkis" (SeaDoo Personal Watercraft), stand-up paddleboards, and kayaks. Tahoe Water Adventures has the equipment and services to meet your needs while on vacation in Lake Tahoe. Take them up on their professional water ski lessons or take one of their scenic tours of Lake Tahoe by boat.

Tributary Whitewater Tours
10068 Hirschdale Rd. Truckee, CA 96161
Whitewater rafting trips near Lake Tahoe, from 1/2 day 3+ days on the Truckee, American, Yuba, Carson and other rivers. For all levels, from family vacation trips suitable for kids from 4 years, to rafting adventures for the expert. Reliable water flows all summer long!! Over 30 years of safe fun trips on many California rivers. List of nearby and Northern California tours:

Truckee River Rafting
175 W River Rd. Tahoe City, CA 96145
CLOSED until the river is running again.
Truckee River Rafting, Tahoe's original raft company! Family owned and operated since 1973. Experience a day on the Truckee River you won't soon forget! Launching from Tahoe City, you'll float along five miles of the serene Truckee River, landing at the River Ranch pond. Our commercial grade 2, 4, 6, 8, and 10 person rafts are top of the line

providing for a safe and easy rafting experience. Along the relaxing, self-guided trip through tranquil waters, you'll experience scenic meadows, wild life, mountains and some small rapids. Each trip takes approximately 2-3 hours so be sure to bring along a small cooler with some snacks and drinks, (please no glass or Styrofoam). Don't forget the sunscreen! Truckee River Rafting is fun for all ages (2 years and up) and will provide lasting family memories for years to come. When you are done head over to River Grill in Tahoe City for some great food and drinks!

Get $5 Off Per Person! With advanced reservation online or by phone (530) 583-1111.

- ✓ FREE Kids 2-5 years old
- ✓ FREE Parking
- ✓ Return Shuttle Bus, Paddles & Vests included
- ✓ Group Rates Available
- ✓ Operating Daily 8:30-3:30. Last bus at 6pm.
- ✓ Early Bird Rates from 8:30-9:30am
- ✓ No Time Limit On Trip (runs approx. 2-4 hours)
- ✓ Finish At River Ranch Pond, shuttle returns to Tahoe City.
- ✓ Souvenir Photos Available, view after your trip!
- ✓ Commercial Rafts Hold Up To 10 People

✓ Footwear Mandatory

Camping and RV Parks

Come discover the wonderful North Lake Tahoe camping and RV parks dotted along Tahoe's north shore and Truckee. One of the most perfect Tahoe campground is General Creek Campground at Sugar Pine State Park with their 175 campsites, great facilities and nearby activities. Meeks Bay Campground offers a lakefront setting where walking to the beach is a breeze. Some campers prefer Kaspian Campground with it's close proximity to Tahoe City and Sunnyside. With the stunning blue waters of Lake Tahoe as your backdrop camping is an outdoor adventure your family will remember for years. Whether you are RV camping or hitting the backcountry, camping at Lake Tahoe will bring you closer to mother nature herself.

You will discover there are many Lake Tahoe campgrounds run by the California State Parks (800-444-7275) and the U.S. Forest Service (800-280-2267) call to reserve your spot today.

D.L. Bliss State Park, Lester Beach

Lake Tahoe South West Shoreline. CA 96142
Lester Beach and Calawee Cove Beach are located at D.L. Bliss State Park have to be some of Lake Tahoe's most awe inspiring beaches with expansive views of Lake Tahoe. The park location is on the West side of Lake Tahoe, just above Emerald Bay. D.L. Bliss State Park covers

1,830 acres and includes some six miles of magnificent Lake Tahoe shoreline with a popular trail that is worth every step. Although Lester Beach and Calawee Beach are not as expansive as some, they offer more private coves with excellent views. The beach areas are integrated with the camping sites, so visitors claim their piece of the beach early. Beach access can require a little stair navigation in spots, but worth the short treck. Arrive early because the beach parking lot can fill up fast and in case the beach is full check out these other Lake Tahoe beaches that are nearby.

D.L. Bliss State Park Campground
At D.L. Bliss State Park camping is the main draw, with family campsites featuring a table, cupboard and stove, nearby restrooms, and hot showers. There are no hook-ups, but some sites will accommodate 15-foot trailers or 18-foot motorhomes. The group site fits up to 50 people and up to 10 cars. For a little adventure, try one of the 20 primitive campsites that are only accessible by boat. D.L. Bliss State Park campground is on Tahoe's west shore so you might consider it to be a South Lake Tahoe campground or North Lake Tahoe campground the distance there is split.

Boaters can use boat launching facilities about 6 miles of the north or south of the park. Another favorite activity is fishing for Rainbow, Brown and Mackinaw trout, and Kokanee salmon. Lake Tahoe hiking is another draw with many trails to explore, including the Rubicon Point promontory which allows you to see over 100 feet into Lake Tahoe's crystal clear depths. Dogs are allowed in the park, but are not permitted on the trails or beaches. D.L. Bliss State Park is located 14 miles north of South Lake Tahoe, CA and 17 miles south of Tahoe City on Highway 89.

General Creek Campground at Sugar Pine State Park
Off Hwy. 89 South of Tahoma.Tahoma, CA. (530) 525-7982
Bring your tents, trailers, and motorhomes! Sugar Pine Point State Park's General Creek Campground has 175 campsites, each with a table and stove, plus nearby restrooms, showers, and a sanitary dump station. There are 7 wheelchair friendly campsites as well as a paved path for walking, biking and wheelchair use. Family campsites can fit up to 8 people and 3 cars, while group sites can fit up to 40 people and 10 vehicles. Dogs are allowed on a leash in developed areas of the park, but are not permitted on park trails.

This pleasant Lake Tahoe campground is nestled in a beautiful forest setting with lots of shade and enough space between campsites to give you a fair amount of privacy. Enjoy the paved bike bath that winds through the forest campground and then heads north into Tahoe City, CA, where you have access to stores, groceries and more beaches!

There are plenty of hiking and biking trails to be found, and in the winter months there is a maze of cross country skiing trails in the park area. Less than a mile away is the Edwin L, Z'Berg Natural Preserve, Hellman-Ehrman Mansion/Pine Lodge, and the Sugar Pine State Park beach and lakeshore area. This historical area will add a magical moment to your vacation, so take an afternoon and relax along the shores of Lake Tahoe's west shore.

Directions: Sugar Pine Point State Park and General Creek Campground is found 9 miles south of Tahoe City, CA, on Highway 89 and 18 miles from South Lake Tahoe (with access to the nearby beach)

Kaspian Campground
Just off Highway 89 on Barker Pass Road. CA. (530) 543-2600
Kaspian Campground is located on the west shore of Lake Tahoe between Meeks Bay and Sunnyside. You will find the campground is located right off of Highway 89 on Barker Pass Road. There is an RV (Campground Host) just inside the entrance. You will park here and carry your camping gear into the sites. Kaspian Campground offers easy access to the lake shore so you can enjoy the beach and water access. It is also not as busy since the idea of carrying your gear in keeps some campers away. Campsites range from partial lake views some more private spots surrounded by the pine forest.

Directions: Kaspian Campground is located on the west shore of Lake Tahoe on Highway 89, near Tahoe City, California.

Lake Forest Campground

Lake Forest Road, East of Tahoe City. Tahoe City, CA 96145
Lake Forest Campground is located one and a half miles east of Tahoe City, off Highway 28 on Lake Forest Road. Lake Forest Campground consist of 20 sites that are available on a first come, first serve basis. The sites themselves are set along a looping road that lacks a thick forest setting, but makes up for it with thick bushes and grass which creates a nice privacy barrier at most sites. Many consider Lake Forest Campground as more of an overflow area when no other campsites in the area are available. The location makes it a nice North Lake Tahoe campsite with it's close proximity to Tahoe City, the Truckee River and Kings Beach. For boaters you can launch your boat at the Lake Forest Public Boat Ramp in the same location as the campground. The campground is run by Tahoe City Public Utility District.

Directions: Lake Forest Campground is located one and a half miles east of Tahoe City, off Highway 28 on Lake Forest Road.

Meeks Bay Campground

Near Tahoma. CA. (530) 543-2600
Meeks Bay Campground is ideally located on the south end of Meeks Bay with a wonderful Lake Tahoe beach to spend your summer days

lounging and swimming. Choose from 40 tent and RV campsites (accommodates RV's up to 20' long). The campground has a nice setting with smaller pines for shade and large shrubs to provide some privacy. The campground is not too large so overcrowding and noise is not as much of an issue. The only drawback at the campground would be some road noise for campsites that skirt along Highway 89 (Emerald Bay Road). The easy walk to the beach is a major plus. There are standing BBQ's and fire rings at all sites and the campground does provide water, BBQ rings, and flush toilets. There is also easy access to Meeks Bay Resort and Marina right next to the campground offering boat launch, water craft rentals, store, snack bar and other amenities.

Directions: Meeks Bay Campground is located on Highway 89 approximately 10 miles south of Tahoe City and 8 Miles North of Emerald Bay, on the west shore of Lake Tahoe.

Mt. Rose Campground
Off Mt. Rose Hwy 431. NV. (877) 444-6777
You will find Mt. Rose Campground to be one the higher campgrounds around Lake Tahoe at an elevation of 9,300 feet. It's in a wonderful high elevation wooded setting with many great boulders that add to the mountain charm. The sites are clean and the newer roads make it one of the more up date campgrounds. A lot of time and attention has been put into this Lake Tahoe campground with picnic tables on

cement slabs that help keep the dust down as well as steps to site locations where needed.

There are 20 single and 5 double-family sites and one triple-family site for larger groups. The Mt. Rose Campground offers restrooms, picnic tables, food storage lockers and fire rings and well as potable water. Many campers like the easy access to area trails including Tahoe Meadows Trail, Tahoe Rim Trail, Mount Rose Wilderness Trail and Mount Rose Summit Trail. It is also an quick 5 mile drive into Incline Village, Nevada where you have access to groceries, gas, restaurants and Lake Tahoe.

Directions: Off Mt. Rose Highway 431 take the Mt. Rose Campground entrance into the campground

Fishing and Charters
No matter what the season, it's time to fish at Lake Tahoe. Grab a pole and let the expert North Lake Tahoe fishing guides lead you to the hottest fishing spots on the lake. You are sure to come ashore with a whole string of mackinaw, rainbow trout, brown trout and kokanee salmon. Whether you are on the lake or hitting one of the many local streams, this is your chance to come home with a fishing tale that even your kids will be bragging about.

Check out Mickey's Big Mack Charters at Sierra Boat Company in Carnelian Bay. Mickey Daniels is a master fishing guide with 45 years of experience and has a sport fishing boat equipped with the latest in electronics and gear. Book a private and personal charter with Captain Chris' Fishing Charters. Captain Chris will guide you to some of Lake Tahoe's best kept secret fishing holes and will even fillet your catch for you when you get back to shore.

Fishing is a fun way to spend the day with family and friends, and there are many great Lake Tahoe fishing charters ready to outfit you and get you on the water with ease. You are sure to come back with a pile of fish to enjoy and stories to tell. There's nothing more relaxing than a day spent hunting for the biggest catch of them all. Make Lake Tahoe fishing a part of your vacation plans.

Captain Chris Fishing Charters
Tahoe City, CA 96145. (530) 583-4857 Local
Captain Chris' Fishing Charters offers year-round Lake Tahoe fishing charters and is easily accessible from North Lake Tahoe, Truckee and Reno. You will find Captain Chris does it all, from taking your reservation to filleting your fish whether it be Lake Tahoe's Mackinaw or Rainbow trout. Captain Chris' Fishing Charters are his 25 foot Skip jack with a comfortable cabin and restroom. All of the charters are private, all of the time!

Chuck's Bait, Tackle & Guide Service
8545 North Lake Blvd. Kings Beach, CA 96143

Chuck has been fishing the Lake Tahoe area for over 40 years. Come fishing with Chuck on his 28' Baha Cruiser. Enjoy the enclosed cabin and restroom while you're not out catching fish on big deck. Morning fishing rips includes coffee, hot tea or yummy hot chocolate to warm from the inside out. Two trips Daily. Call for times and reserve your Lake Tahoe fishing charter today! Get your fishing licenses onboard and save time. Play your own tunes with his iPod/iPhone docking station and enjoy a great day of fishing on Lake Tahoe year-round.

Kingfish Guide Service
5190 West Lake Blvd. Homewood, CA 96141. Homewood, CA 96141 Kingfish Guide Service has you fishing in style on their boat "The Kingfish," which is a 43 foot cabin cruiser designated and constructed specifically for service on Lake Tahoe. The Kingfish is fully equipped to accommodate 40 passengers. Activities are somewhat seasonal. Fishing charters are offered year-round and there is also a daily Emerald Bay cruise on summer afternoons. You can also book a private party fishing charter as well as personal or group cruise, wedding, cocktail party, etc.

Mickey's Big Mack Charters
5146 North Lake Blvd. Carnelian Bay, CA 96140
Mickey's Big Mack Charters is located at Sierra Boat Company in Carnelian Bay. Master fishing guide Mickey Daniels, brings his knowledge and 45 years of experience to give you one great fishing

experience. Mickey Daniels has been featured on Fishing the West, Country Sportsman, Fishing Getaways, Angler West, California Angler, Sunset Magazine and Outdoor Life. Hop aboard the spacious 43' Big Mack II sportfisher. It was designed specifically for Lake Tahoe, equipped with the latest in electronics and fishing gear. Enjoy your day fishing for deep lining for Mackinaw, Rainbow and Browns.

Sierra Fin Addicts Guide Service
PO Box 4267. Incline Village, NV 89450
Whether you are a novice fisherman or a seasoned veteran — you've come to the right guides. Sierra Fin Addicts Guide Service specialize in shallow water and light tackle applications for Mackinaw, Rainbows and Browns. Fishing Lake Tahoe isn't just a hobby to these guides, it's an addiction. Sierra Fin Addicts Guide Service offer both open and private fishing charters on Lake Tahoe. Both prime time morning and afternoon half day trips are available year-round, weather permitting. These trips run 5 hours dock-to-dock. Three-quarter day private charters are also available.

Thy Rod & Staff
12611 Hillside Dr. Truckee, CA 96161
Frank R. Pisciotta is one of California's top fly fishing guides. In 1984 he established his Thy Rod & Staff guide service to help other anglers learn the craft and fish the greater Lake Tahoe area. Frank offers The Reel School of Fly Fishing and other clinics to fit your needs. He can

also offer private clinics tailored to your specific desires, skill levels and schedule. Learn from a local professional who has fished the many streams and rivers of Northern California.

Golf Courses

Challenge yourself! Discover world-class North Lake Tahoe golf courses that are one in a million, from the amazing views and clean mountain air to the professional services and fantastic amenities. These are among the most scenic courses in North America, offering a unique golfing experience. Best of all, there are plenty of golf courses in Lake Tahoe to choose from. So clean those clubs and get swinging.

Consider navigating the acres of stately pines and blue sagebrush at Old Greenwood Golf Course, a Jack Nicklaus Signature Golf Course. You may just have your best game yet at the secluded Coyote Moon Golf Course with its rolling hills, enormous granite outcroppings, delicious sent of wildflowers, and beautiful Trout Creek gurgling in the background. You might take on the challenge at the Resort at Squaw Creek Golf Course, a Robert Trent Jones Jr. championship golf course, nestled at the base of Squaw Valley USA. Another popular golf venue is Northstar Golf Course, with its blend of majestic pines and partial valley for a one-of-a-kind experience.

Clean mountain air, rolling greens, sparkling Lake Tahoe, and unbeatable services come together to create a recipe for your best game yet. Of course you can continue the challenge at one of the South Lake Tahoe golf courses. You haven't experienced golf until you've experienced golfing at Lake Tahoe.

Tahoe Donner Golf Course
12850 Northwoods Blvd. Truckee, CA 96161
18 Holes | Par 72 | Yardage 6,917

Located just minutes off Interstate 80 in Truckee, Calif., the Tahoe Donner Golf Course is one of the premier public golf courses in the high Sierra. This 18-hole, 7,002-yard par-72 championship golf course is located on 200-acres of pristine Sierra landscape with towering pines featuring stunning views and meandering creeks, granite rock formations, elevations changes and greens so consistently pure they have been recognized as the "Best Greens in the Tahoe Region." Tahoe Donner Golf Course is a true mountain course where golfers can enjoy the peace and quiet of the natural surroundings for an incredible value

Coyote Moon Golf Course
10685 Northwoods Blvd. Truckee, CA 96161
18 Hole | Par 72 | Yardage 7177

If you are looking for one of the most scenic golf experiences in the country, consider Coyote Moon's 250 acres of rolling hills, towering pine trees, wild flowers, magnificent granite outcroppings, and crystal clear Trout Creek. This course is truly secluded with not a home in sight to spoil the view. Let the clean mountain air refresh your senses as you focus on a challenging 18-hole game.

Designed by former PGA Tour player Brad Bell, Coyote Moon is a test to golfers of all levels. Expect a few forced carries, many tee shots with ample landing areas, and holes that are well protected by trees, sand, and water. There is a pro shop onsite, practice facilities, and a bar and grill. The course is located in historic Truckee, California, and a mere 15 minute drive from Lake Tahoe.

Incline Village Championship Golf Course
955 Fairway Boulevard. Incline Village, NV 89451
18 Holes | Par 72 | Yardage 7,106

Incline Village has two championship golf courses that are world renowned for their spectacular Lake Tahoe views and challenging greens. The more expensive of the two is the Incline Village Championship course. It was originally designed by architect Robert Trent Jones Sr. in his classic, yet distinctive style, and was completely renovated and updated in 2003. Players will discover this course not only demands accuracy and a hard drive, but creativity as well. The Championship Course was voted onto Golf Digest Magazine's "Best in State" list and was listed among Golfweek Magazine's "Best Courses to Play in 2011."

The fairways are tightly cut and bordered by towering pine trees. You can expect bunkered greens and lateral water hazards on almost every hole. Improve your game at the state-of-the-art practice facilities, get advice from PGA and LPGA professionals, or hang out in the Chateau Club House with its golf shop and restaurant. Rent an electric golf cart equipped with GPS and take advantage of the snack bar and bar carts on the course. The Incline Village Championship Golf Course's mountain layout is exquisite to say the least and is considered a true masterpiece.

Incline Village Mountain Golf Course
690 Wilson Way. Incline Village, NV 89451
18 Holes | Par 58 | Yardage 3,519

Incline Village has two championship golf courses that are world renowned for their spectacular Lake Tahoe views and challenging greens. The Incline Village Mountain Course is the more affordable of the two and a very fun challenge as well. Designed by award-winning golf course architect Robert Trent Jones Jr., the mountain layout with its towering old growth trees makes it a very scenic 18-hole course. The course was actually carved out of a pine forest and has no artificial landscaping making it a continual challenge to all skill levels. You can expect elevation changes, and remarkable green sites and contours. The terrain can be tricky to navigate and will demand accuracy more than distance. The course is a par 58 and takes about 3.5 hours to play. Visit Incline Village Mountain Golf Course for a unique golf experience.

Northstar at Tahoe Golf Course

168 Basque Drive. Truckee, CA 96161. (530) 562-3290./ (866) 628-0418 Event Cordinator
18 Holes | Par 71 | Yardage 6,097

The vibrant and exciting Northstar at Tahoe Golf Course is stunning! Renowned golf course architect Robert Muir Graves designed it to combine the mountainous landscape with the Martis Valley's open meadow. He created two distinct 9-hole courses that each has a challenge in store for you. The courses wind seamlessly through tall pine trees using the natural terrain to create a challenging game. The Meadow Nine (holes 1-9) starts with a links-style course where you can drive hard and perfect your low accurate shots. The Mountain Nine (holes 10-18) will require a bit of creativity to make it through the tree-lined fairways and small greens. If you are looking to improve your game, the resort has a driving range and offers adult, family, women, and junior golf lessons. Northstar also has a beautiful full-service clubhouse and pro shop, and sports bar. Located near Northstar and Truckee, California, this course is one of Lake Tahoe's best resort golf experiences. Open daily, May 18 through mid-October from 7:30 a.m. 6:00 p.m.

Weddings and Speical Events

Northstar California™ Resort, located between Lake Tahoe and Truckee, is an exceptional setting for your Lake Tahoe wedding. Whether you're looking to get married on our Golf Course or prefer the majestic mountain for your wedding backdrop, we offer year-round options for your unforgettable wedding. Our full service catering department that can cater your wedding reception as well as your rehearsal dinner or "after glow" brunch. Our wedding coordinators are ready to offer expert assistance and help you with the little details on your big day.

Old Brockway Golf Course
7900 North Lake Blvd. Kings Beach, CA 96143. (530) 546-9909
9 Holes | Par 36 | Yardage 3,420

Among the plethora of golf courses near Kings Beach is the historic Old Brockway Golf Course, designed by renowned Scottish architect John Duncan Dunn. Featuring tight fairways and lush greens, it was rated a Top Ten Golf Course by Golf Today magazine and was the location of the first Bing Crosby Golf Tournament in 1934. Golfers can challenge themselves with more than 3,400 yards, including two par 5 holes. Amenities include a clubhouse, pro shop, practice facilities, putting green, and driving range. Old Brockway was the first 9-hole course in the US to become an Audubon Cooperative Sanctuary. Grab your clubs and reach a new height of relaxation as you enjoy the majestic views and meander through the towering pines at Old Brockway Golf Course.

Old Greenwood Golf Course
12915 Fairway Drive. Truckee, CA 96161
18 Hole | Par 72

Old Greenwood is a true gem of a course! This world-class Jack Nicklaus Signature Golf Course was rated among the "10 Best New Public-Access Courses in the Country" by Golf Magazine and placed fourth among "America's Finest New Upscale Public Courses" by Golf Digest magazine. There is nothing that quite compares to Old Greenwood's acres of immaculate greens interspersed with stately pines and blue sagebrush. The 18-hole course is simply stunning with the natural landscape incorporated into the course. Old Greenwood is also surrounded by a planned community with gorgeous homes.

If you have young golfers or want to improve your own game, sign up for The Golf Academy at Old Greenwood. It offers junior camps, private and group lessons, and customized corporate sessions. Book a two-course special at Old Greenwood and its sister course, The Golf Club at Gray's Crossing, which is right across the street. Receive a warm welcome from the friendly staff, check out the golf shop, relax in the clubhouse, and finish off your day at the Terrace Grill. Any way you look at it, Old Greenwood offers an excellent golfing experience.

Weddings and Special Events

Let the professionals at Old Greenwood Golf Course host your next big special event, banquet or wedding. Choose from three wonderful venues in the Truckee/North Lake Tahoe area which include Alpine Club, PJ's at Gray's Crossing and Schaffer's Camp. The Sierra Mountains offers a beautiful serene setting and nearby Lake Tahoe an endless outdoor playground for guests.

Ponderosa Golf Course

10040 Reynolds Way. Truckee, CA 96161
9 Holes | Par 35 | Yardage 3,022

Nestled in the pines just outside of Truckee, California, is a remarkable little golf course with well-maintained greens the pose and challenge to all skill levels. Ponderosa Golf Course is a 9-hole course with 3,018 yards and a par of 35. It was designed by prolific golf course architect Bob E. Baldock in 1961. The NCGA rated course is fairly flat and flanked by ponderosa pine trees, while challenging sand traps are placed strategically throughout the course.

Rates at Ponderosa are more affordable than some of the other courses in the area. Family owned and operated since 1963, Ponderosa Golf Course has a friendly and accommodating staff standing by to help you with all your golfing needs. Although there is no driving range here, there are golf cart rentals, a pro shop and snack bar. Tee off at Ponderosa this season!

Resort at Squaw Creek Golf Course

400 Squaw Creek Rd. Olympic Valley, CA 96146
18 Holes | Par 71 | Yardage 6931

For a truly unique links-style course, head to the Resort at Squaw Cree Golf Course. This little piece of paradise is surrounded by six majestic mountain peaks, making it one of the most breathtaking courses in Lake Tahoe. It is located at the base of Squaw Valley USA and offers 18 holes of championship golf and a par of 71.

After 10 years of extensive planning, the course was designed by renowned golf course architect Robert Trent Jones Jr. in such a way as to preserve the natural landscape, wetlands and wildlife habitats of the Squaw Valley. The result is a high-quality, environmentally conscious golf course that is recognized by Audubon International as a Certified Cooperative Sanctuary. Squaw Creek is considered extremely challenging to beginners and experts alike who must focus on accuracy rather than distance. Squaw Creek Sports golf shop is onsite, and lessons, golf carts, and valet parking are also available.

Tahoe City Golf Course

251 N. Lake Blvd, Tahoe City, CA 96162
9 Holes | Par 33 | Yardage 2,691

The lush, evergreen-lined Tahoe City Golf Course is in a municipal setting and one of the least expensive courses in the area. It offers 9 holes and is a great place to practice the basics. The relaxed staff is courteous and helpful. Golf carts are available, as well as a driving net, restaurant and sports bar.

This public course has a rich history and was originally built in 1917 by May "Queenie" Dunn Hupfel. In the 1950s this course was frequented by famous individuals such as Frank Sinatra, Bing Crosby, Dean Martin, Bob Hope, the Mills Brothers, Ken Venturi, Andy Williams, Harvey Ward, and Sammy Davis Jr. Today, Tahoe City Golf Course is the host of the annual Two Bills Memorial Golf Tournament, which has raised more than $200,000 for the Tahoe City Little League program over the last 10 years. Check out the Tahoe City Golf Course for a different kind of golfing experience.

Tahoe Hiking

Challenge yourself! Go experience a real adventure! Let the natural beauty of Lake Tahoe surround you! North Lake Tahoe hiking is a once-in-a-lifetime opportunity to see some of the most amazing natural wonders in the world. Begin with a 5-mile journey to Marlette Lake, which starts at Spooner Lake and leads uphill through the scenic North Canyon. This hike hooks up with popular Flume Trail, one of the most well known and most requested biking trails at Lake Tahoe.

Maybe you have been wanting to treck Lake Tahoe's most popular Tahoe Rim Trail. The 13-mile Rim Trail North and the 12-mile Rim Trail South both offer great views of the Carson Valley and glimpses of crystal clear Lake Tahoe. Take the Mt. Rose hike challenge and sign the log book at the summit to make it official. Mt. Rose is one of the highest peaks near Lake Tahoe, and you can expect excellent views of the lake, Washoe Valley and the City of Reno.

There are many Lake Tahoe hiking trails to choose from, so lace up those hiking boots, lather on the sunscreen and head off for an adventure into unspoiled wilderness. You will be rewarded with beautiful scenery, glimpses of area wildlife, lungs full of pure mountain air, and a feeling of accomplishment that cannot be matched. There are South Lake Tahoe hiking trails as well suited for any ability and skill level, and best of all are the memories of the area's natural beauty that will draw you back again and again.

Brockway Summit to Watson Lake
Watson Lake Rd. (Park top of Broakway Summit) CA
Distance: 13.4 miles round trip

Elevation Change: 7000 ft. to 7760 ft.

Hiking Watson Lake Trail:
Casual hikers love Watson Lake for it's beauty and seclusion. It is a perfect site for a picnic and swim with gorgeous views, wildflowers, and small wildlife. The trail is more of a scenic path on fairly flat terrain for the first 4.5 miles then a gentle climb for 2.2 miles to Watson Lake. A small area of the path can be a bit soupy until it dries

out in the later part of summer. On the trail you will come across forest service roads, specifically Fiberboard Freeway (FSR 73) and the Tahoe Rim Trail meets up with the road in several locations. The hike is not ideal for young kids because of the length of the hiking trail. You can drive into the lake if you prefer and enjoy other trail offshoots along the way.

Optional Biking Route—Mt Watson Road to Watson Lake:
Bikers enjoy riding up the road that leads to Watson Lake. This a moderate to difficult trail for most riders. The road is fairly isolated, smooth trail making it a fun ride to the lake. Expect some moderately difficult climbing with some fast descents, and one steady 2.2 mile climb that will give you a good workout. You will pass over several streams before reaching the lake. Relax and unwind before heading back or you can continue on the main Mt. Watson road which continues on toward Tahoe City and eventually turns into a dirt road.

Directions: To get to Watson Lake from Downtown Truckee, CA, head east onto Brockway Road, and turn right onto Brockway Road (Highway 276)—this will take you up Brockway Grade. Brockway trailhead is on about 0.5 miles south of Brockway Summit. Park and start your journey to Watson Lake

Desolation Wilderness
Stretches up the west side of Lake Tahoe. CA. (530) 543-2600

Directions to Trailhead: There are several ways to access Desolation Wilderness. One fairly popular access point is by Echo Lakes. Take Highway 50 to Echo Summit and turn onto Johnson Pass Road. Stay left and the road will lead you to the parking area by Lower Echo Lake.

Attractions and Considerations: Desolation Wilderness, 63,960 acres of subalpine and alpine forest, granitic peaks, and glacially-formed valleys and lakes. It is located west of Lake Tahoe and north of Highway 50 in El Dorado County. Desolation Wilderness is jointly administered by both the Eldorado National Forest and Lake Tahoe Basin Mgnt. Unit.

At Echo Lakes there is a boat taxi operated in the summer by Echo Lakes Resort cuts three miles off your trip. A fee is charged for this service. Contact the Echo Lakes Chalet for more information: (530) 659-7207. If you prefer to hike around Echo Lake then the trail head is marked at the marina area. A wilderness permit is required. Day hikers, pick up your permit at the self serve area at the trailhead. Overnight hikers will need an overnight permit for Desolation Wilderness. This permit must be purchased before you get to the Echo Lakes Trailhead. Visitors can reserve overnight permits online by visiting www.recreation.gov.

West Side Trailheads (Eldorado National Forest) : Loon Lake Trailhead, Buck Island Trailhead, Van Vleck Trailhead, Rockbound Trailhead, Twin

Lakes Trailhead. Lyons Trailhead, Pyramid Creek (Twin Bridges) Trailhead, Ralston Trailhead, Echo Trailhead

East Side Trailheads (Lake Tahoe Basin Management Unit) : Echo Lakes Trailhead, Glen Alpine Trailhead, Mount Tallac Trailhead, Bayview Trailhead, Eagle Falls Trailhead, Meeks Bay Trailhead

Emigrant Trail
Hwy 89 (Start at Donner Picnic Area). Truckee, CA 96141
This is Truckee's most popular mountain biking trail, but is also a great hiking trail worth exploring. Truckee's Emigrant Trail offers stunning scenery, mellow rolling single-track, the perfect early-season biking warm-up what's not to love about the Emigrant Trail? Beginner and intermediate riders alike can hit this trail in early spring as it is one of the first trails to lose its winter snow. Families adore this trail, groups with differing skill levels find it a great compromise, and beginners find it a boost to their skills and confidence.

Most rider (or hikers!) start at the Donner Party Camp Picnic Area parking lot and the image gallery showcases this starting point. Right from the start the trail runs parallel to the north side of Prosser Creek. After you leave the creek, expect to cross a number of dirt roads. Don't worry; the main crossings are well marked and the minor crossings are obvious. Enjoy rolling hills on this out-and-back adventure, with very few minor technical spots. The uphill runs are minimal, but you can still enjoy some fast sections through open valleys. Enjoy swimming in the Stampede Reservoir to cool off in the summer months. In May and June enjoy beautiful wildflowers while the mountain scenery is guaranteed to be stunning year-round.

Starting from Downtown Truckee, heading northeast on Donner Pass Rd., you will come to the roundabout where you merge onto SR 89N. Continue about 4.5 miles to the Donner Camp picnic area located on the right.

Emigrant Trail is popular on the weekends and at the peak of the tourist season, making it a little crowded the first mile or two. Total riding time is just over 2 hours. In the early spring the trail can be a bit muddy in parts. If you are looking to gain a deep love of mountain biking, ride this trail once and you will be hooked.

Glenshire Lake
Glenshire Clubhouse. Truckee, CA 96161
Nestled among alpine peaks of Truckee, the Glenshire Lake loop is relaxing and simple to navigate, making it perfect for families with young children. This area has lots of gently rolling hills and gorgeous mountain views. Part of the scenic trail crosses a lush meadow of wildflowers as it circles around the quaint lake on gentle terrain. Take an evening stroll in the soft glow of a gorgeous sunset, or enjoy your walk under the twinkling stars. Dogs on a leash are welcome. For

something more challenging visit the North Lake Tahoe hiking trails directory.

Directions: To get to the trailhead from downtown Truckee go east on Donner Pass Road, take a right on Glenshire Drive and drive 5 miles to the Glenshire Clubhouse parking lot (on the left). The trailhead is behind the clubhouse.

Bikers Please Note: Glenshire Drive is not biker friendly due to a lack of shoulders and high speeds.

Prey Meadows / Skunk Harbor
On west side of hwy 28, 2.25 mi north of 28/50 junction. Incline Village, NV
Directions to Trailhead: Take Highway 28 from Highway 50 north approximately 2 miles. Look for an iron pipe gate on the west side of the highway. Park in one of the turnouts along the highway but do not block the gate.

Trail: Snow free in early spring, this is a great walk through a mixed conifer forest with filtered views of Lake Tahoe along the way. When you reach a fork in the road, you have two options. The left fork leads to Prey Meadows which is blanketed with many varieties of wildflowers in the spring. The right fork leads you to Skunk Harbor, a small picturesque cove which offers great swimming and sunbathing in the summer.

Attractions and Considerations: Look for the remains of an old railroad grade along the way, built in the 1870's as part of the network to supply timber to Virginia City

Sawtooth Trail
Off US Forest Service 06. Truckee, CA 96160
This adventure takes mountain bikers, runners, and day-hikers along the ridge between Squaw Valley and Northstar ski resorts. Many Truckee local's like to bike the Sawtooth Trail for a fun excursion that is not too difficult. The gentle rolling single-track trail snakes through some rocky, sparse forest areas. The elevation gain tops off at 500 feet, and while most of the track is smooth dirt there is a challenging section with a lot of scree deposits. It is recommended that you take the trail counterclockwise, so that you descend on this loose rock area instead of climbing up through it. Points of interest along the trail include two overlooks into the Truckee River Canyon that offer gorgeous views of the Truckee River. This trail also connects with other routes on the Mt. Watson network of trails if you choose to make this a more difficult or extended mountain bike ride. Check other North Lake Tahoe biking and hiking trails nearby like the Watson Lake trail.

Directions: The Sawtooth Trail is located in the South part of Truckee, CA, along Highway 89 that heads south of Lake Tahoe. To get there from the center of Truckee, head east on Brockway Road (Highway

267) going towards Northstar Resort, turn right on Palisades Drive, then turn right on Silver Fir, and then left on Thelin Road. Turn right on US Forest Service 06 and drive about ½ mile to the Sawtooth trailhead (on the right). Old forest service roads intersect the trail many times, but if you stick to the single-track it is easy remain on course.

Tahoe XC, Tahoe City
925 Country Club Drive. Tahoe City, CA 96145
Winter at Tahoe XC

Discover serene meadow trails, challenging hills, and a few thrilling downhill areas at Tahoe XC in Tahoe City. The setting is ideal for cross country skiers and snowshoeing enthusiasts of all abilities. Its 22 trails, spanning more than 65 km, sport stunning Lake Tahoe views. Nine kilometers of trails are machine groomed daily. Three warming huts offer free hot chocolate and pose as resting spots along the trails.

Tahoe XC is one of the few places in North Lake Tahoe that has dog-friendly trails. The two trails open to dogs and are groomed daily and cover 9 km. They offer PSIA certified instruction, plus rentals for skate, classic, and snowshoe, pull-behind sleds for kids (55 pounds or less), and kids gear. Grab a bite to eat at the Day Lodge Café and enjoy free WiFi. Tahoe XC is host to the start of the Great Ski Race, one of the largest cross country ski events in the western United States, and is located only three miles from the convenience of downtown Tahoe City.

Summer at Tahoe XC

Come in the summer when Tahoe Cross Country in Tahoe City offers trailhead mountain biking as well as bike rentals and more. Enjoy their convenient trailhead mountain bike rentals, food service, retail and repair shop. Tahoe Cross Country offers fantastic trails for beginner and intermediate riders, and there is also easy access to advanced terrain higher up. There is great terrain for all ages and abilities, riding or hiking.

Horseback Riding

Horseback riding in Lake Tahoe is an adventurous way to enjoy this scenic area. Northstar Resort Horseback Riding Stables is perfect for beginners and family groups alike. Their expert guides will lead you over gentle hills and through thick pine forests on horses so gentle that even the most youngest of riders will have a great time. Tahoe Donner Equestrian Center is another great way to explore the Sierra's by horseback. Their wide range of services include lessons for children and adults, and Saturday night barbeques complete with marshmallows to roast and a piñata. There is nothing quite as relaxing as horseback riding through high mountain meadows and over trickling streams to really get your life in perspective

Alpine Meadows Stable
355 Alpine Meadows Rd. Tahoe City, CA 96145

The location of the Alpine Meadows Stable started in the mid 1940's as a pack station and was the first operation in Alpine Meadows, then known as Deer Park. Here the hunters would pack up supplies and ready their horses before for heading into what now called Granite Chief Wilderness. In 1967 Alpine Meadows Stables was purchased by the Courtney Family. Today the Courtney Family keeps the horseback riding tradition alive by offering scenic guided horseback trail rides through National Forest and Wilderness lands. You and your family will enjoy a wonderful day outdoors with a little excitement and beautiful Sierra Nevada Mountain views.

Tahoe Donner Equestrian Center
15275 Alder Creek Rd. Truckee, CA 96160. (530) 587-9470 Local
Young or old, Tahoe Donner Equestrian Center offers a wide variety of horseback riding options. You will find their wide range of services will meet the needs of most recreational horseback riders. Book a lesson for the kids or take one yourself. On Saturday nights join the BBQ and indulge in a customized gourmet burger while you watch the kids play dress up, roast marshmallows and take a swing at the piñata. Tahoe Donner Equestrian Center invites you to come explore the Sierras by horseback. You will gaze in awe at the forests and high mountain meadows filled with wild flowers. Maybe even catch a glimpse of the local wildlife in action

Verdi Trails West Ranch

175 Trelease Lane. Verdi, NV 89439. (888) 345-7603 Toll Free
Verdi Trails West Ranch is the place to start an enjoyable, relaxing trail ride that winds through Their 3000 deeded acres in the Sierra Nevada Foothills just East of Truckee about a 15 minute drive. Trail rides are available year-round for ages six and up. Verdi Trails West also offers spring and summer horsemanship day camps for those who want to learn how to or brush up on their horseback riding skills. Book a Hay Wagon Ride, featuring their team of Belgian Draft Horses, by appointment for groups of nearly any size. BBQ's are available too for parties and large group events.

North Lake Tahoe Marinas

North Lake Tahoe marinas are located from Sunnyside to Sand Harbor and with most marina locations, parking can fill up quickly in the high peak summer months of July and August. Choices include your standard boat launch locations to full service marinas offering fueling docks, deli, convenience store, boat rental and other watercraft rentals. Several Lake Tahoe marinas also offer buoy (mooring) space for the summer so you have quick an easy access to your boat.

Kings Beach State Park and Boat Launch

8318 N. Lake Blvd., Hwy. 28. Kings Beach, CA 96143
Welcome to Kings Beach, the largest public beach on the North Shore! Explore its nearly 700 feet of shoreline or spend the day on the water

with a rental from North Tahoe Watersports. Rent a Jet Ski, kayak, water bike, or paddle boat, or enjoy a parasailing ride or private lake tour. Swimmers claim Kings Beach has one of the warmest beaches on Lake Tahoe do to the fact that it is south-facing and has a gradually deepening lake floor. There is a parking fee, but walkers and bikers can use the beach at no charge. Kings Beach also has the only public dog friendly beach on the North Shore so bring your pooch and your doggy bags.

Enjoy a stroll on the walking paths that meander throughout King Beach Plaza and its patio-style courtyard. It is the site of many special events, including the summertime arts and crafts fairs. This beach is dialed with bathrooms, a basketball court, volleyball courts, horseshoes, barbeque and picnic areas, and a lakefront playground. The recreation area is in downtown Kings Beach, just off of Highway 28.

Coon Street Boat Launch

Boaters can head to the Coon Street Boat Launch, which has restrooms and parking for vehicles with or without trailers. Expect separate fees for launching and parking, which is limited. Coon Street Boat Launch is located at the south end of Kings Beach State Park with easy access to North Lake Tahoe..

Hours for Coon Street Boat Launch: 7:00 AM 7:00 PM, Thursday Monday (Closed Tuesday and Wednesday)

Meeks Bay Marina

7941 California 89.Tahoma, CA 96142

Meeks Bay Marina offers two boat ramps, 120 boat slips, ski boat, canoe and kayak rentals. Coming for the day? Take a special boat tour or rent from their large selection of water skis, wake boards, paddleboats, water toys and accessories. The boat slip area is nicely protected with quick access to Meek's Bay and Lake Tahoe. Take out the boat and cruise up to Sunnyside Restaurant or down to beautiful Emerald Bay. Find a secluded cove and relax! Don't have a boat? Then just come hang out at Meek's Bay beach with other great amenities to make your Lake Tahoe day perfect.

- ➢ 2 Boat Ramps
- ➢ 120 Boat Slips
- ➢ Ski Boat Rentals
- ➢ Canoe and Kayak Rentals
- ➢ Guided Fishing Excursions
- ➢ Paddleboats, Water Toys, and Accessories

Obexers Marina

5300 B W Lake Blvd. Homewood, CA 96141

Obexer's Boat Company, located on Lake Tahoe's west shore, has been a family-owned business since 1948. Obexer's Boat Company if a great facility providing boat launch, travel lift and forklift launching, slip and buoy season rentals, summer and winter storage, repairs on site, boat sales, and chandlery. Launch your boat from one of Lake Tahoe's most beautiful shorelines just minutes away from the popular lakefront Sunnyside Restaurant and Lake Tahoe's famous Emerald Bay.

- Boat Ramp
- Fuel dock with Regular fuel only
- Docks, Slips and Moorings
- Pump out station
- Boat storage
- On Site repairs
- Restoration shop
- Restrooms

Sand Harbor Boat Ramp
Incline Village, NV. (775) 831-0494

Launch your boat into one of the most scenic spots on Lake Tahoe. Sand Harbor boat ramp is a favorite location since there is quick access to some of the most beautiful beaches on the Tahoe's north shore. It is a smooth easy boat ramp with beach access right near the launching area and then there is nearby Sand Harbor beach with extra amenities. Sand Harbor boat launch offers two wave protected double ramps with docks and adjacent parking. Get there early during the summer peak months since parking is limited. The parking lots are often full from 11 a.m. to 3 p.m. on summer weekends and weekdays during July and August. Watercraft inspections are required as part of the new program that is helping to protect Lake Tahoe from the threat of aquatic invasive species such as Quagga and Zebra mussels.

Hours:

Summer May 1 through September 30, 6 am to 8 pm

Winter October 1 through April 30, Friday, Saturday and Sunday only, 6 am to 2 pm. Winters hours are subject to change and/or closure.

Tahoe City Marina and Mall
700 North Lake Blvd. Tahoe City, CA 96145
Tahoe City Marina & Mall offers the very best for boating, shopping and dining on the north shore of Lake Tahoe. The Marina is one of the oldest Lake Tahoe marinas and is full service marina offering a full line of boating and recreational fun. You will find several recreational outfitters including daily parasailing, sailing cruises, kayak rentals and various fishing charter boats. Marina services include boat rentals, slip and buoy rentals, indoor winter boat storage, forklift and travelift, launching (no public ramp) and fuel sales. Located in a historic building that is headquarters to the Tahoe Yacht Club which host the annual Lake Tahoe wooden boat show "Concours d'Elegance."

- Boat launch (no public ramp)

- Fuel dock with regular fuel
- Docks, slips, and moorings
- Pump out station
- Restaurant and shopping
- Restrooms
- Repair facility nearby
- Boat sales, rentals and storage

Tahoe Vista Recreation Area and Boat Launch
7010 North Lake Blvd. Tahoe Vista, CA 96148
Tahoe Vista Recreation Area and Boat Launch underwent a total reconstruction that was completed in the summer 2006. Come enjoy the beach and picnic area on the 2.7 acre lakeshore property, with approximately 800 feet of lakeshore frontage. The Recreation Area includes lake access, a sheltered boat launching facility, picnic area, restrooms, sidewalks, and a large plaza area with interpretive signage. This is a Tahoe Vista local's favorite so come get out on Lake Tahoe or catch some rays on the beach. One of North Lake Tahoe's more quaint beaches to discover and the boat launch is easy to navigate.

Outdoor Sports

Hiking in South Lake Tahoe

So you want to go hiking in South Lake Tahoe. You checked in to your room or suite, or even perhaps the five bedroom deluxe vacation cabin, at the 3 Peaks Resort and Beach Club, unpacked your bags, and have partaken of the mandatory meandering about the town. You walked the two short blocks to our private beach, took off your shoes, and walked barefoot in the sand. You walked the two blocks to the base of the Heavenly Gondola, checked out the Heavenly Village shops, perhaps wandered the two or three blocks to one of the casinos just over the line in Stateline, Nevada. But none of those are the real purpose of your trip. You're here to get away from all that. You're here to experience the wonderful wilds of the South Shore of Lake Tahoe.

So, what's available in the way of hiking trails around here? There are seven highly popular and relatively well traveled hiking trails in the South Lake Tahoe area you will want to know about and possibly explore. As is customary we'll begin with the easy, walking trails and work up through the more strenuous. The most difficult trails are covered in another article: Advanced Hiking in South Lake Tahoe.

There are three well-known easy walking trails: Moraine, Angora Lakes, and Lake of the Sky. All three of these trails are relatively flat; the Lake of the Sky Trail at the Lake Tahoe Visitor's Center is the shortest at 1/3 mile one way. The Angora Lakes Trail is about 1/2 mile. Once at the lakes you can swim or do some fishing. As the lakes are quite popular you will want to get there early to "reserve" a spot if you intend to spend the day. The Moraine Trail is a beautiful nature walk of about a mile (one way) through a forest and along the shoreline of Fallen Leaf Lake.

A moderately difficult, and much longer, hiking trail is Echo Lakes. This trail is great if you don't know exactly how hard you want to work for your pleasure! A short 2-1/2 mile hike brings you to the northwest corner of Upper Echo Lake. Other lakes, requiring longer treks, include Tamarack Lake (about 1-1/2 miles further), Lucille and Margery lakes, and Lake of the Woods (different trails each about 1 mile beyond Tamarack Lake), and Aloha Lake (about a mile from lake of the Woods or Margery Lake). So you can walk until you get "half tired," then turn around and start back. Hike as far as you like and enjoy great lake and forest scenery regardless of how deep you penetrate the wilderness.

Advanced Hiking in South Lake Tahoe

For the experienced hiker South Lake Tahoe offers a number of options depending on how hard you want to work and how long you want to wander in the wilderness. The Glen Alpine Trail is rated "moderate to difficult" and offers numerous options depending on your mood. Grass Lake is two miles from the trailhead. The alpine lakes of Susie, Heather, and Aloha, are 4, 5, and 6 miles respectively along a single route that also includes a small waterfall along the way.

For a really good workout, experienced hikers can choose between the 1-2/3 mile Clark Trail that has a steep grade, loose shale, and the

Upper Angora Lake as a payoff and the Mt. Tallac Trail. The first half of the Mount Tallac Trail, past Floating Isle and Cathedral lakes, is not strenuous. Beyond Cathedral Lake, the trail heads right up the face of Mt. Tallac and is about 3,000 ft. above the trailhead. We're talking potentially significant changes in weather. A windbreaker, plenty of water, and careful scheduling so as to leave time for the return trip, are all considerations on this hike. The views of Lake Tahoe, Fallen Leaf Lake, and the Desolation Wilderness are magnificent. The entire route from trailhead to mountain top is 5 miles (one way).

When planning your hike remember to comply with USDA Forest Service regulations. If you are only going to be on the trails during the daytime, you can usually get a Wilderness Permit at each trailhead. If you plan on camping, however, it's necessary to visit the Forest Service Visitor Center where you can not only get the permits you need but maps, brochures, and no doubt sage advice. Nobody knows the trails and terrain like the Forest Service, and visitors are encouraged to pick their brains before heading out.

Winter Sports

Lake Tahoe winter sports are one of the main reasons people visit the region between mid-November and April. Tahoe is one of the west coast's most popular ski vacation areas. Snowfall in the surrounding mountains is the heaviest of any winter recreational area in the United

States. Most winter visitors come for the downhill skiing and snowboarding, although cross country skiing and snowshoeing are growing in popularity. There are so many resorts nestled in the mountains around Lake Tahoe it's difficult to keep track of them all. Lake Tahoe winter resorts can best be grouped by geography.

South Lake Tahoe

Heavenly Ski Resort is practically within the city limits of South Lake Tahoe, sits atop Monument Peak in the Sierra Nevada Mountain Range, and is the most conveniently located resort on the southern rim of the lake. There are vast numbers of hotels and lodging nearby. A gondola whisks visitors directly from town to peak. Kirkwood is about 35 miles south of South Lake Tahoe on Carson Pass, and Sierra-At-Tahoe in Twin Bridges is just 18 miles southwest of the city. Oh, and incidentally, in South Lake Tahoe, if you want a hotel, you should know that you can easily walk from the 3 Peaks Resort and Beach Club to the lake, the mountains (via the Heavenly Gondola), and the casinos.

North Lake Tahoe

North Lake Tahoe, being much closer to Reno and its airport has a number of accessible resorts. Alpine Meadows, Boreal, Diamond Peak, Mt. Rose, Squaw Valley, and Tahoe Cross Country are well-known resorts in the North Lake Tahoe area.

Truckee and Donner Summit

In the general area of Truckee and Donner Summit there are Northstar-At-Tahoe, Royal Gorge (cross country), Soda Springs, Sugar Bowl, and Tahoe Donner. Sugar Bowl, being west of the Sierra Crest is a good choice if you want to easily beat the afternoon rush hour traffic.

Weekend Crowding

Most of these resorts have high speed lifts, plenty of lodging, and large crowds, especially on the weekends. But Alpine Meadows, Diamond Peak, and Mt. Rose on the northern side of the lake are less crowded. Sugar Bowl and Homewood near Donner Lake aren't as busy, and the crush of cattle both Sierra-At-Tahoe and Kirkwood is less of a problem. Resorts to the west of the Sierra Crest are the closest to the Bay Area and Sacramento, so skiers wanting to make a quick getaway in the afternoon to avoid the rush hour traffic are advised to consider these areas. Both Kirkwood and Sierra-At-Tahoe fall into this category.

Skiing on the Flat

How about some cross country skiing? Or snowshoeing? The best and cheapest places to work up a sweat are the many trails in the Tahoe National Forest. But, Royal Gorge and Tahoe Cross Country both cater to the "skinny ski" set. The Spooner Lake Cross Country Ski Area is just 12 miles from South Lake Tahoe and Stateline, NV. Whether you're into striding, diagonal stride, skating, telemarking, or snowshoeing, these resorts provide well groomed trails, warming huts, trailside cafes, and a host of amenities designed to take the edge off the rough sport of cross country skiing.

Every Day's Tip: The flatter the terrain, and the slower the chair lifts, the cheaper the "lift" tickets.

Downhill at Heavenly

South Lake Tahoe's Heavenly Resort is reached by gondola from the base of the mountain right in the middle of town. And guess what? The 3Peaks Hotel and Beach Club is practically next door to the Heavenly Gondola and Heavenly Village Shops. With skis slung over their shoulders and snowboards tucked under their arms, 3Peaks hotel guests trudge the two blocks to the base of the Heavenly Gondola every morning during the winter months. This is hard work for the downhill set; perhaps the farthest they'll have to walk under their own power all day long. Nevertheless, those that survive the trek and everyone does are gently lifted along the 2-1/2 mile length of the gondola's route to Adventure Peak at 9,156 ft.

Adventure Peak is where beginners can learn to ski, showshoers can trek about the area, sledding for children under 6 years of age is available, as is supervised tubing, even snow biking. After all that exercise exhausted adventure seekers can kick back at the Adventure Peak Grill and refuel for the next few hours on the slopes. There are ski schools for adults and kids for skiing and snowboarding targeted at all experience levels. Adaptive ski instruction is available for the adventurous disabled as well. Parents will be happy to make use of the day care services and even combinations of day care and ski or snowboard instruction are available. These activities for the most part are centered around the Adventure Peak area. Several lodges are strategically located elsewhere on the mountain for the convenience of weary skiers and riders.

With 30 lifts, 91 trails, a people hauling capacity of 52,000 per hour, with a peak at 10,067 ft., and a vertical drop of 3,500 ft., Heavenly is one of the grandest downhill ski resorts in the country and by far and away the largest in California. But to take full advantage of all that mountain, you'll want to get farther up the hill than Adventure Peak. To do that, take the Von Schmidt trail down to the Sky Deck. Here the Sky Express lift will whisk skiers nearly to the top of the mountain at 10,040 ft. From this point virtually every trail in the resort is accessible. As you face the lake, you can go left along the Ridge Run. Several downhill trails of varied difficulty peel off to the right as you travel to the west along the ridge. If, as you face the lake, you ski to your right or east, you'll find yourself on the Skyline Trail that meanders along until the Milky Way Bowl. From here the California Trail leads to several intermediate trails. The Milky Way, however, takes you down an advanced slope to Killerbrew and Mott canyons where only the most expert skiers and snowboard riders are welcome. Everyday at 3 PM the Ski Patrol sweeps these areas, collecting bodies.

Summer Activities

The many summer activities on and around Lake Tahoe include boating, fishing, swimming, walks along the 71 miles of shoreline, and a whole host of other water based activities. With over 71 square miles of surface area, the lake enables virtually any kind of water activity. Since it's your vacation, whether you want to do your own thing or prefer to take a tour bus, boat, helicopter, or hot air balloon ride, you'll have no trouble finding fun and excitement, relaxation, family outings, even romance, on or by the waters of Lake Tahoe.

Speed about in a motor boat or glide smoothly across the mirror-like surface of the lake in your sailboat. Lake Tahoe is a boating paradise with marinas and boat ramps located on all four sides of the lake. Some lake enthusiasts water ski, wakeboard, parasail, and jet-ski. Others sail, kayak, canoe, or windsurf. Why not head on over to Emerald Bay on the western side of the lake. Here, surrounded by the Emerald Bay State Park, is a quiet refuge from the modern world where nature's natural beauty is on display. Fannette Island in the middle of the bay is the only island in Lake Tahoe. Emerald Falls is visible from the bay as is Vikingsholm Castle, a mansion built in 1929, and considered one of the finest examples of Scandinavian architecture in the western hemisphere.

Mackinaw trout is the best sport fish species in the lake. Technically salvelinus namaycush, but more commonly known as Lake Trout, they are a cold water fish that normally spend the summer months deep in the water to avoid the warmer temperatures near the surface. Other trout found in Lake Tahoe include rainbow and brown. Kokanee salmon is prevalent in the lake as well. Kokanee is the name given to Sockeye salmon when they're confined to fresh water lakes. If sport fishing is your game, you'll be more than happy with the fish of Lake Tahoe.

The Truckee River is the only outlet from Lake Tahoe and white water rafting, fishing, or ATVing along the river banks are some of the more adventurous activities. Picnicking, with and without barbeque grills, sunbathing, walking along the lakefront, building a sand castle; there are parks and picnic areas scattered liberally all along the lakeshore. Instead of a hotel, consider staying at the 3 Peaks Resort and Beach Club. You'll have no trouble walking back and forth between the beach and your room or suite or the mall if you forgot the hotdog buns.

Had enough of the water? Hiking, mountain biking, and horseback riding are all popular pastimes in the Lake Tahoe Basin. Biking trails are quite numerous and all levels of exertion are available from the casual sightseeing trail to the rough and tumble mountain bike challenge. Hiking trails are also found all around the lake and range from a casual stroll to quite strenuous climbs. Follow the Tahoe Rim Trail for 165 miles completely circling the lake. On the western side of the lake lies the Desolation Wilderness, high on the Sierra Crest. Backpackers seeking the unusual will be rewarded with Lake Aloha, Horsetail Falls, and other highly regarded natural wonders.

Biking South Lake Tahoe

South Lake Tahoe biking, for our purposes, can be divided into biking and mountain biking. Despite the recent upsurge in the popularity of mountain biking, many visitors to the Lake Tahoe region still prefer to do their bicycle riding on paved roadways without too many frame bending bumps and drops. Families, especially, find the traditional bicycle paths a great way to get some exercise while discovering both the natural beauty of Lake Tahoe and the many man made sights along the way.

In the neighborhood of South Lake Tahoe, the Pope-Baldwin Bike Path is a paved path beginning at the beach of the same name just to the south of Emerald Bay. Along its 3-1/2 mile route Pope-Baldwin passes Camp Richardson, the Tallac Historic Site where riders are encouraged to stop and tour the area –, and along the shoreline of Fallen Leaf Lake. The route is mostly flat.

The South Lake Tahoe Bike Path, sometimes called the Forest Bicycle Trail, begins at El Dorado Beach in the South Lake Tahoe Recreation Area, or if you follow the South Lake Tahoe Chamber of Commerce's suggestion, it begins at the Crescent V Shopping Center. The path passes over Trout Creek and the Upper Truckee River and passes along the lakeshore ultimately connecting with the Pope-Baldwin Bike Path up near Emerald Bay. The trail is paved with blacktop and passes through a good ten miles of forest. The Baldwin Estate and the Forest Service Visitor Center are both good places to stop along the route for some sightseeing and rest.

If you've thought ahead and are staying at the 3 Peaks Resort and Beach Club, you have probably rented a cabin with a Jacuzzi. So when you complete your ride a moment of relaxation will help you transition from the mountains, the dirt, and the sweat to the perfume, the comfortable clothing, and the evening's entertainment.

Mountain Biking South Lake Tahoe

South Lake Tahoe mountain biking is a great way to work up an appreciation for the comfortable accommodations at the 3 Peaks Resort and Beach Club. After a day of frame bending, teeth chattering, dirt eating ecstasy, nothing beats a soak in your room's tub and a brief nap before hitting the casinos. But first, the ecstasy. Here are three mountain biking trails convenient to the resort and guaranteed to justify that evening soak.

Whether it's called Angora Lakes Climb or Angora Ridge, this biking trail is a great introduction to the mountain biking experience for beginners and a beautiful, relaxing ride for the more experienced. Partially paved and partially dirt, this trail proceeds about two miles to Angora Lookout and then another two miles to Angora Lakes. Along the way, the views of Mt. Tallac and Fallen Leaf Lake are spectacular. In fact, from Angora Lookout the panoramic views of Lake Tahoe and the Desolation Wilderness are magnificent.

Mr. Toad's Wild Ride is a highly technical, dangerous, stomach turning 1,500 ft. descent from the 7,200 ft. trailhead at Big Meadow. Several really rough rock chutes and drops of up to six feet make this a ride for strong-at-heart experts. The 13 mile ride can be combined in a circular route that roughly follows Route 89 south from Meyers towards Luther Pass a bit less than 4-1/2 miles. The trail then winds its way back down to Meyers in some beautiful and occasionally hair-raising back country. Technically, this part of the ride, the hard part, is referred to as the Saxon Creek Trail. If you plan on making the entire circuit, be sure and take along plenty of water as some riders report running out well before completing the circle.

The Flume Trail is located in Lake Tahoe Nevada State Park and is popular enough to be crowded at times. To get to the Flume Trail begin at Spooner Lake, work your way uphill to Marlette Lake, where the trail proper actually begins. Crossing a dam, the trail follows a ridge for approximately 4-1/2 miles and ends at Tunnel Creek Road. This is an expert ride exclusively for those not afraid of heights! Floating 1,300 ft. above Lake Tahoe, the views along this route can be quite distracting. But, then, isn't that at least part of the point?

The Truckee River

The Truckee River is the only outlet from Lake Tahoe. Snow pack on the High Sierras, principally at the southern end of Lake Tahoe, melts and flows into the lake via the Upper Truckee River beginning way up somewhere around Carson Pass. At Tahoe City, the waters of Lake Tahoe flow into the Truckee River which flows west to the town of Truckee, then east through Reno, Nevada, and then north to the southern end of Pyramid Lake.

At the head of the river is the Lake Tahoe Dam with its 17 sluice gates. Back in the very early 1900's, a gatekeeper, or water master, lived at the river's source, charged with managing the flow of water over the dam. The reconstructed gatekeeper's cabin is now a museum housing artifacts from the history of Lake Tahoe. A wonderful collection of Native American baskets representing over 80 different tribes.

The Truckee River is a great place to fish, ride a raft down the rapids, or do some casual sightseeing, all depending on which length of the river you happen to be on at the time. Tourists are gleefully informed of the famed "fanny bridge" or "rump row" which is revealed by sightseers leaning over to look at the river below.

So what kind of fish can you hope to catch in the river? Lehonatan trout seem to be the holy grail of Truckee fishermen, with 20-lb. monsters being common in prehistoric times. Ah, but no more. Today hunters will find the formidable Brown and Rainbow trout to be heavily represented and more numerous. Nevertheless, experienced fly fishermen know that these underwater predators have little interest in becoming your prey and are not easily outwitted.

White water rafting? On the Truckee River? You bet! The river has Class I through Class IV stretches. Beginners and casual sightseers will enjoy the stretch from the Lake Tahoe dam to River Ranch. Just beyond Boca Reservoir, when the Truckee and Little Truckee rivers merge, is where the real fun begins. Class II, III, and IV, rapids are present until rafters reach Floriston. After that rafters will enjoy the ride into Reno.

Downtown Reno, Nevada, has constructed a whitewater park on the Truckee that runs right through the Arts District with its galleries of painting, sculpture, pottery, and furniture. Boutique shops, coffee houses, cafes, and nightlife are all found on the Riverwalk. Extending for half a mile with six drop pools in the south channel and five in the north channel, the park, a kayaker's playground, flows around Wingfield Park, on an island, with facilities for concerts and picnics. The Truckee River, then, continues on its way to the southern end of Pyramid Lake. But that's a subject for another day.

Lake Tahoe Snowshoeing

Lake Tahoe snowshoeing is a great family activity that everyone from the youngest to the oldest can enjoy. Many of the winter resorts in the Lake Tahoe area have groomed trails, warming huts, and even cafes along the trails to refuel. Trails are often used by both snowshoers and cross-country skiers, so a certain amount of trail etiquette is necessary.

Modern snowshoes are fashioned from space age materials like polypropylene, are often solid (without the traditional lattice work), and have hinged heels called ascenders. Solid snowshoes? Yep! It turns out that in the real world of trekking across the snow the worry about snow covering, and weighting down, the snowshoe was groundless. It just doesn't happen! Unlike skiers, snowshoers don't wear ski boots (too heavy) but rather light hiking boots. Most snowshoers use poles similar to ski poles for balancing purposes.

If you're staying at the 3 Peaks Resort and Beach Club, just steps away from the Heavenly Gondola, you'll probably want to start out snowshoeing at the Heavenly Resort's Adventure Peak where up to 4K of snowshoeing and cross-country skiing trails are available. There are even introductory class sessions for newbies. Sierra at Tahoe, located just 12 miles west of South Lake Tahoe, has a groomed three mile snowshoeing trail. Signs along the route describe local flora and wildlife.

Serious snowshoers, who want to cover a lot of territory, will find a tremendous number of trails throughout the Lake Tahoe region. Many of the hiking trails in the Tahoe National Forest are also open in the winter to cross-country skiers and snowshoers. On the South Shore the Echo Lakes Trail is fairly flat and an excellent starter trek for beginners. The Little Round Top trail takes snowshoers along a ridge providing almost continuous scenic views. The Mount Tallac climb is only recommended for those with considerable experience as the terrain rises 3,000 ft. in about 2.5 miles, a fairly steep slope requiring intimate familiarity with one's snowshoes.

Crusing Lake Tahoe

Glide across Lake Tahoe on a wooden sail boat or cruise on a powerful motorboat. Woodwind Cruises has sail boats leaving from both the Camp Richardson and the Zephyr Cove resorts up to five times a day.

Motor boat cruises travel up both the west and east shores of Lake Tahoe. The cruise on the East Shore includes a visit to the Thunderbird Lodge Historic Site where a guided tour reveals the many eccentricities of the original owner. The West Shore cruise reveals the Hellman-Ehrman Mansion of Sugar Pine Point State Park and Emerald Bay with magnificent views of Eagle Falls, Vikingsholm Castle, and Fannette Island.

Two stern-wheelers grace the lake. The M.S. Dixie II, home ported at the Zephyr Cove Marina, and the Tahoe Queen, home ported at the Ski Run Marina both offer a combination of nostalgia and crystal blue water adventure and both take visitors to Emerald Bay.

Tahoe Gal is a modern vessel, christened in 1994, with the look and feel of a side wheeler. Home ported in Tahoe City, this vessel cruises the West Shoreline with its lavish real estate. A separate cruise visits Emerald Bay, passing the Erhman Mansion and Vikingsholm Castle.

The Tahoe Paradise is a super modern luxury motor yacht launched in 1998 and incorporating the latest in nautical technology. The double-decker has a fully enclosed, climate controlled lower salon deck with huge picture windows for viewing the spectacular Sierra Nevada Mountains. The upper deck is open to the sun- or moon-shine and appropriate for lounging, weddings, or dancing.

Other boating options include the Tahoe Cruz, a sailing yacht out of the Tahoe City Marina, and the Tahoe Princess, available for private charter, double hulled, accommodating up to 120 passengers, and home ported at the Ski Run Marina. For speed demons, the Tahoe Thunder is an 800 horsepower catamaran based at Timber Cove Marina.

Lake Tahoe Wakeboarding

Wakeboarding Lake Tahoe is a great way to combine your need for speed with your frustrated inner surfer. Why wait around for the big wave? Why swallow all that salt water? Just get yourself a speedboat and a wakeboard, and practice your butter slides or, if you're a real hot shot, work on your boardslides. With over 192 square miles of surface area, water skiers, wakeboarders, and wakeskaters will have all the necessary trick room to show their stuff.

Wakeboards, for those of you just getting started, are somewhat oddly shaped, but are similar to snowboards in that they are permanently fixed to the rider's boots. Hence, the board is going to follow your feet. They are shaped more like surfboards than snowboards, however, made of plywood or fiberglass, but much shorter. They tend to be somewhat wider in the center than at the ends and are rocker shaped. That is, if you set the board on the ground the center will touch the ground and both ends will not. How deep this bend in the board is is called its "rocker." (You know, as in rocking horse. Get it?) As with all boards with stationary bindings for your feet, riders' toes point to one side of the board and their heels to the other. When describing maneuvers, reference is made to the toeside and heelside edges of the board.

Also, wakeboarding requires a specially outfitted speedboat, usually with a tower from which the line is played out to the wakeboarder. If you didn't bring your own, where can you rent one? At virtually any of the marinas, wakeboards and wakeboarding boats can be rented or purchased. If you like taking lessons, there are ski schools located at several marinas.

The idea is similar to water skiing in that as you are pulled along behind a speedboat you can use the boat's wake to launch yourself into the air, landing on the other side of the wake. This is known as your basic Air Raley. Of course, as one becomes more advanced, all sorts of tricks can be attempted. Fakies, Air Krypts, Surface 360's, Tantrums, Back and Front Rolls, are just some of the colorful names the more common tricks have been given.

So what is wakeskating and how is it different from wakeboarding? The wakeskating board is not attached to your feet with bindings. Rather, an easy to grip material, similar to that used on skateboards, helps keep the rider's feet in contact with the board. Riders wear shoes that provide traction when wet. Wakeskating boards are smaller than wakeboards. Also, when performing maneuvers, riders have to reach down and hold the board adjacent to their feet, much as land based skateboarders do. Wakeskating is somewhat more technical than wakeboarding, requiring a bit more skill getting started.

Lake Tahoe Parks

As one would expect, Lake Tahoe parks are quite numerous. Some of the more obvious parks and recreation areas that travelers will encounter while driving around the lake include D.L. Bliss State Park, Emerald Bay State Park, Sugar Pine Point State Park, Burton Creek State Park, Kings Beach State Recreation Area, and Lake Tahoe Nevada State Park. They are all pretty much right on the lake.

Burton Creek is primarily a hiking and cross country skiing recreational area. The Kings Beach State Recreation Area is primarily a lakefront park popular with visitors engaged in water related activities. Both D.L. Bliss and Emerald Bay are great places for camping with walking trails to spectacular views. If you're into scuba diving, Emerald Bay has a terrifically exciting underwater barge and boat graveyard that is becoming increasingly popular.

There are many other parks and recreation areas in the Lake Tahoe region, most notably, Desolation Wilderness, the Eldorado and Tahoe National Forests, the Mt. Rose Wilderness Area, and Washoe

Meadows State Park. The Pacific Crest Trail (PCT) passes through both the Eldorado and Tahoe national forests.

The Mt. Rose Wilderness Area includes much of the Carson Range's high country. The Reno city limits are close to this area and it is easily accessible from the city. This, no doubt, accounts for the heavy trail usage. Between 100 and 200 hikers a day can be found on the Mt. Rose Trail. Wildlife is plentiful, including mule deer, bobcats, black bears, grouse, and mountain quail.

A number of hiking trails in the Desolation Wilderness beckon. Hikers seeking a moderately strenuous day of adventure will find Meeks Bay Trail quite scenic. Those seeking awesome beauty you have to pay for in sweat will find the Mount Tallac Trail challenging. Other trails in and around the Desolation Wilderness are Bayview, Eagle Falls, and Glen Alpine. The first is difficult and the others are moderate up to a point beyond which they too become more challenging.

Stateline, Nv

As a determined vacationer you will most likely have chosen the 3 Peaks Resort and Beach Club for its ideal location, rustic décor, modern amenities, and superb service. Yet, having spent a day or several on the lake or the mountains, exploring local boutique shops and galleries, or enjoying a fish dinner by the lake, the restless guest with a few extra coins in his or her pocket may want to consider an excursion out of state.

Step across the line to the bright lights of Stateline, Nevada, and into the fantasyland of big time casino action. MontBleu, formerly Caesars, Harrah's, Harvey's, and Horizon are the four largest gambling establishments here, featuring every sort of wagering. Slot and video poker machines are too numerous to count as are the table games, craps, and roulette. That ever popular buffet dining experience is here as well.

MontBleu's casino has slots and video, table games, and The Zone where poker players can find virtually every popular game while keeping up-to-date on world racing and sporting events via huge plasma screens on the walls. Prefer to do one thing at a time? Enjoy a deli sandwich while watching one of the 12, individual 12-inch TV's. MontBleu's fine dining features steak, seafood, and vegetarian dishes complemented by over 300 wines and champagnes. The Unbuffet goes a step beyond the typical buffet offerings.

Catch a show at Horizon's Golden Cabaret or a movie in their Horizon Stadium Cinemas multiplex movie theater. The casino is cozy and friendly while maintaining all the excitement of the larger venues.

Harrah's alone has eight restaurants offering everything from light sandwiches to the finest haute cuisine. The Summit is billed as one of

America's top ten restaurants; it has a magnificent view from it's location on the 16th floor; and, a pianist soothes diners' digestion in the evenings. 900 slots, table games, Keno, baccarat, and poker keep gamblers alert.

Harvey's Cabo Wabo Cantina offers live music and some unique cocktails of an evening. The art of Remington and Russell hang on the walls of the Sage Room Steak House, but it's rock and roll wall hangings at The Hard Rock Café. The casino covers 52,000 sq. ft. with the latest and best in gaming action.

Stateline's in Nevada, and that means you can get married any time you like. Get married in one of the casino wedding chapels or outdoors with the lake and Sierras in the background. If you prefer to plan ahead a bit, hire professional wedding planners to arrange everything for you and your guests.

Golf. Yes, Stateline has one of the better, and pricier, courses on the southern shore of Lake Tahoe. Edgewood is a public course with tree-lined fairways, water hazards, and many sand and grass bunkers. Genoa Lakes Golf Club & Resort, just 5 miles from Stateline, has an 18-hole public course, and its Resort #2, another two miles up the road, also features an 18-hole public course.

Zephyr Cove Stables is a great place to catch a ride on horseback with a cowboy guide and a hot meal. Located just four miles from the heated action of the casinos, the more leisurely pace of national forest land trails and scenic vistas is a great way to get back to nature.

Emerald Bay

Emerald Bay is a natural wonderland of wilderness beauty perched on the western shore of Lake Tahoe, California. The bay itself, like much of Lake Tahoe, is a striking emerald blue. Just floating on the water here is a pleasure. The surrounding wilderness of pines and cedar against the backdrop of soaring mountains confronts visitors with nature's majesty. Eagle Falls empties directly into the bay and is about as picturesque as it gets with powerful granite cliffs surrounded by evergreens.

The heavily wooded Fannette Island floats in the middle of Emerald Bay with its granite core rising 150 feet above the lake. Set atop the highest point on the island are the ruins of the only man made structure: a Tea House erected by the island's owner Mrs. Lora Josephine Knight who was also the principal force behind the building of Vikingsholm.

Vikingsholm was designed by the Swedish architect Lennart Palme who, with his wife, accompanied Mrs. Knight on an architectural "fact gathering" mission in 1928 throughout the Scandinavian countries accumulating ideas. The 38 room "castle" at the head of Emerald Bay is the result. Widowed and divorced, Mrs. Knight spent her winters in

Santa Barbara and her summers at Lake Tahoe where she had a staff of 15. Built in 1929, Vikingsholm was intended as a summer home and Mrs. Knight entertained guests regularly. Afternoon tea was generally served in the library or on the terrace, but, occasionally, in the Tea House on Fannette Island. When visiting Emerald Bay State Park, touring Vikingsholm is a "must."

Before the turn of the 20th century (prior to 1900), many boats and barges were sunk in the bay. As a result, in 1993, Emerald Bay was designated an underwater state park. No, it isn't the beautiful underwater flora that's being preserved; it's a bunch of sunken boats. Nevertheless, visitors will find the history fascinating.

Emerald Bay State Park and D.L. Bliss State Park are side-by-side on the western shore of Lake Tahoe. A half-mile walking trail in D.L. Bliss State Park will bring curious visitors to 130 tons of granite rock teetering on a very small base. The Balancing Rock has been a popular tourist attraction for more than a century. Hiking, biking, fishing, camping, swimming, guided tours, and some exhibits are all available activities.

North Lake Tahoe

What is going on in North Lake Tahoe? This laid back rural community far different from the hustle and bustle of South Lake Tahoe has something for everyone but with a calm ambiance. The north shore of

Lake Tahoe has always been more of a place to take a quiet vacation rather than party around the clock. The north shore of Lake Tahoe is just 33 miles from Reno, NV, and the Reno-Tahoe International Airport. Incline Village, the largest town in North Lake Tahoe is 29 miles to the north of South Lake Tahoe, CA, and Stateline, NV, if drivers head up State 28, on the eastern side of the lake. From the 3 Peaks Resort and Beach Club, it's a short, relaxing drive.

What makes Incline Village stand out a bit from other towns around the lake is its concentration of innovative, high-tech and Internet oriented businesses. Evidently, business people have seen the advantage of living in rural comfort and relative seclusion while instantaneously communicating with their clientele world wide. So, if you are the CEO of a successful business on the Information Highway, you might want to think "real estate" when visiting this end of Lake Tahoe. If not, well, there's plenty to do in town and everything from water sports, mountain trails for hiking and biking, to nearby winter resorts with every conceivable alpine activity available.

There are a number of casinos on the Nevada side of Lake Tahoe's north shore. For instance, the Hyatt Regency Lake Tahoe Resort, Spa, and Casino. And as with many bars, clubs, hotels, and restaurants, in Nevada, Cosby's Grill Pub Casino encourages barflies and gourmets alike to exercise the one armed bandits between rounds or courses. A few miles down State 28 in Crystal Bay, sort of midway between

Incline Village and Kings Beach, CA, the Tahoe Biltmore has a nightclub on site, Breeze, that features DJ's, Karaoke, shows, and the occasional sporting event. The Crystal Bay Club, renovated in 2003, features elegant comfort, HD TV everywhere, and individually tailored ambiance.

Perhaps the most famous, some would say notorious, of the north shore casinos is The Cal Neva Resort in Incline Village at Crystal Bay. Cal Neva started out life in 1926, as the first casino-hotel on the lake. Over the years, including the period of Frank Sinatra's ownership, the resort had its ups and downs. Today, under new ownership, the casino remains an interesting bit of history well worth a look-see by travelers.

Interesting Small Nevada Towns

When you have a moment to catch your breath from all the outdoor and indoor activities of South Lake Tahoe, you might consider exploring some of the region's interesting small Nevada towns. Between Stateline and Carson City there are a number of quaint, sometimes not much more than a wide-spot-in-the-road, small towns. Some may have a rustic café where a few locals and the occasional trucker hang out. Others might have one or two art galleries or antique stores. And once you arrive at Carson City, the capital of Nevada, there are numerous low-key points of interest.

The adventurous will find the Kingsbury Grade of Highway 207, a fun drive over Daggett Pass. Once you've descended into the Carson Valley, you'll have a decision to make: take the (more) scenic route left, up Foothill Road, Highway 206, through Genoa, connecting with State 395 N, via Jacks Valley Road, or continue on 207, to Waterloo Lane and Highway 88. Traveling north on 88 brings you to Minden, then Bridge House, and finally Carson City. If you take the scenic route up 206, you'll wind your way to Genoa.

Originally settled by Mormon traders in the early 1800's, Genoa (Gen-NO-a) is a town on Highway 206 in the Carson Valley. Walley's Hot Springs is a mile or so to the south. A few miles north of Genoa travelers will find the Genoa Golf Club & Resort where 36-holes of quite challenging golf await the adventurous. Those seeking a gastronomical adventure will find that Antoci's fine Italian dining is superb. In late September The Candy Dance festival is held by the town of Genoa. Arts and crafts are sold to benefit the local town government. Genoa has several antiques stores, art galleries, and

If you decide to drive north on Highway 28, either to circle Lake Tahoe, a popular and satisfying excursion, or to visit Carson City, you'll pass Spooner Lake. Spooner Lake is stocked with trout, has many excellent picnic areas, and is the jumping off point for numerous backcountry trails.

Carson City, named for Kit Carson, is about 25 miles from Stateline, and is reached by driving north on Highway 28, to Spooner Lake and then northeast on Highway 50, to State 395. Originally a silver mining boom town benefiting from the 1859 discovery of The Comstock Lode, and a pony express station, it was designated the capital of the Nevada Territory in 1861.

Carson City has a number of museums including The Nevada State Museum, The Nevada State Railroad Museum, The Children's Museum of Northern Nevada, and The Nevada State Library & Archives. The Capitol building is open to the public and the central business district downtown features a number of antique stores, art galleries, gift shops, and restaurants. And, yes, there are casinos in Carson City. Most include restaurants, bars, nightclubs, and entertainment.

Tahoe's Western Shore

Lake Tahoe's western shore is sprinkled with wilderness areas, beaches, many attractions, small towns, and real estate developments. Old money and new has vacationed on Lake Tahoe's western shore for a hundred years or more. The legacy of yesterday's elites is preserved in such attractions as Vikingsholm Castle and Ehrman Mansion.

Traveling west on Hwy. 89, visitors will pass near the Tallac Historic Site, Fallen Leaf Lake and Cascade Lake, before arriving at Emerald Bay

State Park. With pristine beauty, numerous trails, Vikingsholm Castle, Fannette Island, and Eagle Falls, visitors can easily spend several days enjoying the park's natural beauty.

Continuing north on Hwy. 89, along the mountainside through D.L. Bliss State Park with its Balancing Rock. Rubicon Point in D.L. Bliss is one of Tahoe's more popular scuba diving spots. Meeks Bay is the next significant town you will encounter. Tahoma is next, and located next to Sugar Pine Point State Park with its forests of pine, juniper, aspen, and fir trees. Wireless Internet is available here within 200 ft., of the Carriage House so visitors can stay connected while connecting with the surrounding wilderness or fishing the incredibly clear General Creek. The park has an excellent Nature Center.

Tahoe City is situated at the head of the Truckee River. The Lake Tahoe Dam and the Gatekeeper's Cabin Museum are here as are the Tahoe City Golf Course and Burton Creek State Park. The Truckee River provides plenty of recreational fishing, kayaking, and rafting. Hiking and cross-country skiing are facilitated in the nearby Burton Creek State Park by six miles of unpaved roadways.

The western shore of Lake Tahoe has numerous campgrounds with and without various amenities like RV hookups. They include: Camp Richardson, Fallen Leaf Lake, Emerald Bay State Park, D.L. Bliss State

Park, and Sugar Pine Point State Park, among others. In general, reservations are recommended for all of these campgrounds.

Lakes of South Lake Tahoe

The lakes of South Lake Tahoe, while dwarfed by the much larger Lake Tahoe, are beautiful, cold, often deep (and sometimes shallow), and have interesting developmental histories. Most were carved out by glaciers during the last Ice Age. There are many large and small that can be reached via a short hike in summer and by snowshoe or cross-country skis in winter. Your best source of information is the Forest Service, of course, but here's an introduction to several of the larger and more popular destinations. All of the trailheads from which these places are reached are within a few miles of the 3 Peaks Resort and Beach Club.

Fallen Leaf Lake is about one mile south of Lake Tahoe and is reached by a single lane road, Fallen Leaf Road. There are wide spots in the road to allow vehicles to pass in each direction. The road intersects Highway 89 about 5-1/2 miles to the west of downtown South Lake Tahoe. The lake is almost 3 miles long (north-south) and almost 1 mile wide (east-west). Despite the rather limited access via the single lane road, there are a number of private residences on the lake, most with boat docks. This is a great area to have a picnic or do some hiking. Wakeboarding, water skiing, and fishing are popular lake activities.

The community of Echo Lake is about 12 miles south of South Lake Tahoe. The Lower and Upper Echo lakes are actually connected by a narrow body of water which is, however, only passable when water levels are high. In the winter the area is highly popular with cross-country skiers as the terrain is moderate and access from South Lake Tahoe is easy. Snowmobiles are never allowed except for local residents. The Echo lakes are one of the preferred starting points for summer hikers, winter showshoers, and cross-country skiers to hike or glide into the Desolation Wilderness. To do that however, depending on how long and far you intend to travel, you may need a Wilderness Permit which you can obtain from the Forest Service. Avalanches are a real problem in this area, so again, check with the Forest Service and be aware of your surroundings.

Lake Aloha, Suzie Lake, Heather Lake, Horsetail Falls, Grass Lake, and Gilmore Lake are all accessible by visitors via hikes of under six miles from the Glen Alpine Trailhead (take Fallen Leaf Road from Highway 89) or Echo Lakes Trailhead (Highway 50 south to Echo Summit then onto Johnson Pass Road). Also, you might want to check out Tamarack Lake and Triangle Lake. In all cases, if you're not already familiar with the local terrain and weather, it is recommended that you contact the Forest Service at the Taylor Creek Visitor Center.

Other Things to Do in South Lake Tahoe

Sure folks visit South Lake Tahoe because of the lake, the mountain, and the nearby casinos, but is that all there is? Of course not! There are a number of other things to keep one busy and entertained. Here's a very brief overview of some of the more obvious, and pleasurable, choices.

Golf Courses

In the summer Tahoe's many excellent golf courses are packed and a number of them are in and near South Lake Tahoe and Stateline. Lake Tahoe Golf Course is an 18-hole, public course with panoramic views and tall trees lining the fairways. Tahoe Paradise Golf Course has 18-holes, is public, hilly with trees lining the fairways, and has enough doglegs to keep players thinking. Both are on Emerald Bay Road. Bijou Municipal Golf Course on Fairway Drive has an easy 9 holes, but does require occasionally paying attention to course management. And those are just the local public courses. There are many more fairways, public and private, sprinkled about the Tahoe Basin.

Camping, and Ice Hockey

If you brought the entire family you might find a few hours spent at the South Lake Tahoe Recreation Area fun. With an NHL regulation sized ice arena, an indoor-outdoor swimming pool, gymnasium, weight room, and more, the Recreation and Swim Pool Complex is a great place to burn calories. And there is a campground too. Cabin rentals, RV hookups, and campsites with and without electricity are available.

Of course, before I got myself a cabin, I'd want to check out the prices and amenities at the 3 Peaks Resort and Beach Club.

Tallac Historic Site

From the 1890's through the 1920's this area at the base of Mount Tallac was where the upper crust came to relax and party. A spring-loaded dance floor, boat rides, and gambling were some of the attractions, as now, that attracted the rich and famous of Northern California to the Tallac Resort's two hotels and casino. Some built estates near the action. Today three of these estates remain in various capacities, along with the ruins (harrumph, archeological remains) of the Tallac Resort. Not only can visitors tour the estates, but the Valhalla Boathouse Theatre is the site of concerts, Shakespearean plays, and more contemporary productions.

A Museum at Lake Tahoe

The Lake Tahoe Historical Society Museum isn't probably what you were thinking of when you made your hotel reservations. Nevertheless, it's definitely worth a look see. A "toll booth" from 1859, and numerous historical artifacts make the museum a very different experience from the other activities you'll most likely be engaged in.

Why South Lake Tahoe?

Why South Lake Tahoe? Why not North Lake Tahoe? Or Tahoe City? What's so special about this vacation town on the southern rim of the lake? If you're driving from Sacramento, CA, it's a good 105 miles. From San Francisco, it's 188 miles. If you fly into Reno, NV, it's a 60 mile drive to the far side of the lake. Truckee and the Donner Summit ski resorts and hotels are about 103 miles from Sacramento, and that highway is an Interstate. So obviously something other than proximity to population centers and travel convenience must be involved. What would make people want to spend their vacation time in South Lake Tahoe?

First, there is the obvious fact that, however difficult it may be to get here, once you're here a strategic reservation, say at a hotel or resort like the 3 Peaks Resort and Beach Club, puts you right smack dab in the middle of more action than could possibly be healthy for fragile human beings. Visitors can exhaust themselves in and on the lake itself. They could bring their own boat, or rent one, and do a bit of fishing, boating, or skiing. Or, they could swim, walk along the beach, or build a sand castle. Heavenly Mountain beckons to those needing a good cardio workout. There is plenty of skiing and snowboarding in winter, hiking or biking in summer, on and around the mountain. Or, for those who prefer concentrating on a more isolated muscle group, the hard-core athletes can work their biceps pulling slot machine levers in a Stateline casino any time of year. And all of these things can be enjoyed by visitors to South Lake Tahoe without ever getting in their car or waking up their limo driver. That's right, South Lake Tahoe combines all three of the major reasons vacationers vacation in Lake Tahoe, and in a compact area.

Let's review. Visitors visit Lake Tahoe because of (1) the lake, duh, (2) the mountains, and (3) the Nevada casinos. South Lake Tahoe is the one place in the area where the combination of natural geography and entrepreneurial development has created what is arguably an optimal human playground. Those are the big three attractions, but there is more, much more. That, however, will have to wait for another day and article.

Heavenly Village Shopping

One of the easiest things a visitor can do when getting on or off the Heavenly Gondola at the bottom of the mountain is to stop and shop in Heavenly Village. Sly of those resort architects wasn't it, putting the gondola right in the middle of all those retail establishments? Sly architects or marketing gurus aside, professional shoppers and browsers will appreciate the acquisition efficiency embodied in this place.

Did he, or she, win the argument? Was he, or she, in the right? Well, then, let him, or her, apologize with a little something from one of the jewelry stores here. The Gold Store also has gems. Poe Rava Gem Company and Rock Your World both have unique offerings in stone, gold, and silver. Perhaps an item or two from Sealed With A Kiss?

So you bought a little vacation cabin on the lake? Now you have to put something on the walls? Michael Godard's art, and that of some of his friends, might be just the thing. Or get one of your own framed at Sun Art. If you need a sculpture for the garden, wander into Wyland Galleries. Not sure just what you want? Browse through Tahoe Country to get some ideas.

Forgot to pack the little black dress? And, he's taking you out to The Summit at Harrah's? Relax, scoot into Cache and try on something flirty, or perhaps classic. No, you're in the wilderness (really?), so maybe something more like sporty would be appropriate. Today's woman will be sure to find something in tune with her thoughts in this trendy boutique.

Little black dress indeed! You need blue jeans, a flannel shirt, and one of those denim jackets with fake lamb's wool on the inside. Try High Chaparral Clothing or the Great Outdoor Clothing Company. If high tech outerwear is what you want, teleport into Helly Hanson, Patagonia @ Heavenly, or Quicksilver.

Want to keep the kids busy or buy them those items they forgot to pack? Put them in skates at the ice rink, give them some quarters and point them towards The Village Arcade, or see if they have their size at The Treehouse. If all else fails, buy them tickets to a movie at the 8-plex cinema.

Shopping in South Lake Tahoe

The clear, blue lake; the Heavenly Mountain; the magnificent, high-rise casinos: yes, they're probably the main reason you came to Lake Tahoe. Yet as every dedicated consumer knows, even in the natural, if somewhat tamed, wilderness of South Lake Tahoe it's possible to fill your days with unrestrained, multi-venue shopping. Visitors will find numerous boutique shops, galleries, and restaurants with open invitations to enter and browse, buy, or consume. Shopaholics take note: what follows is a mere suggestion of what is available in and around Lake Tahoe.

Mountain Outlet Shopping

Why else would anyone go to Lake Tahoe, other than to shop? As all professional browsers know, nothing beats a good factory outlet mall and South Lake Tahoe has two. Tahoe Factory Stores on South Lake Tahoe Blvd., and Factory Stores at the Y right at the junction of highways 50 and 89 are the places to shop for name brand items at discount prices. O.K., maybe you can't walk to the Y from the gondola, but you could stop by on your way into town.

Heavenly Village

Heavenly Village is a European styled commercial "mall" surrounding the lake end of the Heavenly Gondola. Cobblestone walkways, and the slopped alpine roofs of upscale boutique shops selling clothing, summer and winter sporting equipment, books, and wine, can divert even the most dedicated outdoorsman from the beckoning mountain. Galleries offer imaginings made real by local artists. Eateries offering gourmet pizzas, tortilla wrapped sandwiches, or sushi, are complemented by Marriott's Fire+Ice. Here the familiar concept of the Mongolian barbecue or Fuddruckers' build-your-own hamburger has been expanded to include an array of seafood, meats, pastas, and vegetables. Diners pile their own ingredients and sauces on a plate and then a Grill Chef applies the heat necessary to finalize the process. Mmmmm!

Browsing the Year Around

Visitors needn't limit themselves to Heavenly Village as there are mini-malls everywhere and restaurants, and shops, and art galleries. In the summertime visitors can stroll from one retail establishment to another. In the winter the reason for all those sloping roofs becomes apparent and getting around in your car is problematic. Hey, there's snow on the ground! Where you want to be moving about is on Heavenly Mountain, preferably with skis, a snowboard, or possibly a pair of snowshoes. Even so, you'll be walking past the same boutique shops, eateries, and galleries. Don't worry about your boots, they're used to that.

Shopping in South Lake Tahoe

The clear, blue lake; the Heavenly Mountain; the magnificent, high-rise casinos: yes, they're probably the main reason you came to Lake Tahoe. Yet as every dedicated consumer knows, even in the natural, if somewhat tamed, wilderness of South Lake Tahoe it's possible to fill your days with unrestrained, multi-venue shopping. Visitors will find numerous boutique shops, galleries, and restaurants with open invitations to enter and browse, buy, or consume. Shopaholics take note: what follows is a mere suggestion of what is available in and around Lake Tahoe.

Mountain Outlet Shopping

Why else would anyone go to Lake Tahoe, other than to shop? As all professional browsers know, nothing beats a good factory outlet mall and South Lake Tahoe has two. Tahoe Factory Stores on South Lake Tahoe Blvd., and Factory Stores at the Y right at the junction of highways 50 and 89 are the places to shop for name brand items at discount prices. O.K., maybe you can't walk to the Y from the gondola, but you could stop by on your way into town.

Heavenly Village

Heavenly Village is a European styled commercial "mall" surrounding the lake end of the Heavenly Gondola. Cobblestone walkways, and the slopped alpine roofs of upscale boutique shops selling clothing, summer and winter sporting equipment, books, and wine, can divert even the most dedicated outdoorsman from the beckoning mountain.

Galleries offer imaginings made real by local artists. Eateries offering gourmet pizzas, tortilla wrapped sandwiches, or sushi, are complemented by Marriott's Fire+Ice. Here the familiar concept of the Mongolian barbecue or Fuddruckers' build-your-own hamburger has been expanded to include an array of seafood, meats, pastas, and vegetables. Diners pile their own ingredients and sauces on a plate and then a Grill Chef applies the heat necessary to finalize the process. Mmmmm!

Browsing the Year Around

Visitors needn't limit themselves to Heavenly Village as there are mini-malls everywhere and restaurants, and shops, and art galleries. In the summertime visitors can stroll from one retail establishment to another. In the winter the reason for all those sloping roofs becomes apparent and getting around in your car is problematic. Hey, there's snow on the ground! Where you want to be moving about is on Heavenly Mountain, preferably with skis, a snowboard, or possibly a pair of snowshoes. Even so, you'll be walking past the same boutique shops, eateries, and galleries. Don't worry about your boots, they're used to that.

South Lake Tahoe Eateries

It is not the case that the number of South Lake Tahoe eateries exceeds the year around population of this resort town. But, one could be forgiven for thinking so, as there are a large number of dining choices. Let us begin with the finest of the fine.

Most of Stateline's casinos have one or more relatively elegant, gourmet restaurants where the chefs are considered artists rather than cooks. When diners are expected to savor the presentation as well as the sauce, we can safely assume the experience has ascended above mere enjoyment and entered the realm of the sublime.

The Summit at Harrah's Lake Tahoe serves a to-die-for Pistachio Encrusted Rack of Lamb and the Cipollini Onion Soup will warm up your palette beforehand. The Sage Room Steak House atop Harvey's will light your fire with a tableside flambé. And be sure to order the Bananas Foster for dessert to ensure a proper ending to the fireworks display!

David Lofgren, formerly of Spoon, Butterfly, and Hawthorne Lane in San Francisco, has settled into the kitchen at Evans American Gourmet Café on Emerald Bay Road in South Lake Tahoe. Is this cozy cabin that serves up entrees as "roast Cervena venison loin on roast butternut squash with caramelized apple compote and shaved Brussells sprouts with panetta" really the best restaurant in all of Lake Tahoe? Is his wife, Sarah, the Master Pastry Chef, equally talented? If you'd like to find out for yourself, reservations are recommended.

Perhaps you just want a bite to eat in a more casual atmosphere? Then try Ernie's Coffee Shop on Emerald Bay Road near the airport for breakfast or lunch. Or, go south of the border at Chevy's Fresh Mex Restaurant on Lake Tahoe Blvd. Carina's Café & Deli and Heidi's Restaurant are also on Lake Tahoe Blvd. Want live music with your American barbecue? Check out Hoss Hoggs. Or, you could ride the Heavenly Gondola up the mountainside to the Monument Peak Restaurant where the view competes with the American cuisine for your attention.

There is still more. McDonalds or Pasquale's Pizza in South Lake Tahoe; The Chart House on Kingsbury Grade in Stateline; and Rojo's Tavern on Hwy. 50 in South Lake Tahoe are also likely to appease the hungry wilderness dweller. There are restaurants in marinas with views of the lake and in shopping malls with views of the parking lot. Virtually every ethnic cuisine is represented in one or another South Lake Tahoe restaurant. So don't be afraid to work up an appetite on the mountain or the lake, because the eateries of Lake Tahoe are ready to refuel you for another day.

Lake Tahoe Antiques

Doesn't everyone come to this wilderness playground with antiquing in mind? Lake Tahoe antiques: there's more than you might think. After all, when you think about opening an antique store don't you want to be where the antique buying public hangs out? What are people going to do when they've exhausted themselves skiing behind a boat or down a mountain? Go antiquing, of course!

Let's start our travels through the used, overused, and restored furniture and knick-knacks strewn about this shopper's paradise in South Lake Tahoe. South Lake Tahoe Antique & Thrift Company is right on South Lake Tahoe Boulevard. Zephyr Cove, Nevada, has several antique, and thrift, stores that should interest the curious perhaps after a round of golf at Edgewood Tahoe in Stateline. There's Sierra Paniolo Trading and Cherry Hill Antiques, both on Dorla Court.

Practically next door to the Tahoe City Golf Course in the Boatworks Mall is the Hemmings & Jarrett Home Store which specializes in home furniture and accessories. Girasole on West Lake Blvd., Tahoe City Antiques on North Lake Blvd., are also worth a browse. On Interstate 80, midway between Donner Lake and Truckee, you'll find The Donner Trading Company and Jordan's Collectibles. If you're going skiing up that way anyway, why not stop in and see what they have on display? Better yet, check out European Ski Antiques on Truckee Tahoe Airport Road. They've got a great selection of antiques and antique skis and sleds as well.

Driving on up to the north end of the lake will bring travelers to Kings Beach, on the California side of the border. Front Porch Antiques on

North Lake Blvd., is the place you'll want to stop and see here. Incline Village, across the border in Nevada, is where you'll find Yours Again, a consignment shop with style and elegance.

Now, if you're willing to travel a bit farther afield, you'll find even more antique stores in Carson City and Reno. As those who are passionate about antiques of all kinds know, it's as much about the search, browsing wherever that particular piece might be hiding, as it is about finding the right object for that spot in the room or on the wall.

Lake Tahoe Weddings

A Lake Tahoe wedding is the choice of many couples who want to tie the knot in beautiful, natural surroundings. Lake Tahoe is a bucolic paradise conveniently located just a few hours from the major west coast population centers. Not only can you have your dream wedding in the wilderness, but all of your friends and relatives can easily get here for the blessed event; there is plenty of lodging; and when the reception is over and the couple has left on their honeymoon, guests can hang around for a day or two enjoying the lake and mountains.

If you "Google" something like "Tahoe wedding," you might just be overwhelmed with the possibilities! There are wedding chapels, ministers, planners, photographers, florists, even wedding packages with all the details skillfully wrapped up with a single price tag. There are venues in both California and Nevada; there are indoor places often with great views and outdoor spots against spectacular backdrops; and every hotel, casino, restaurant, and bar with seating for 25 or more would love to host your reception. One place where you can find information concerning a host of wedding related details fairly easily is the Tahoe's Best Wedding Guide at http://www.tahoesbest.com/Weddings/. They have information on wedding dresses, cakes and caterers, beauty salons, getting a marriage license, and more.

When you are doing your planning, keep in mind the fact the 3 Peaks Resort and Beach Club in South Lake Tahoe is happy to accommodate large groups. Why not have your invited guests all stay here where they can interact, getting to know one another, without the crush of so many other visitors. You and your guests can experience the rustic ambiance of our grounds, the sandy lakeshore, the mountain heights, and the convenience of the largest town on the shores of Lake Tahoe. And they can do it together as a group rather than searching for familiar faces in the larger, more crowded venues. Give us a call at (800) 331-3951.

Relaxation at The Beach Club

Lake Tahoe vacations are usually about winter or summer sports, gambling at a Nevada casino, or perhaps a wedding or honeymoon.

But there are other reasons for traveling all the way up here from wherever, and perhaps the most appealing is to just get away from it all. Turn off the cell phone, unclip the beeper, turn off the Blackberry ®. O.K., you can use your laptop to read this article if you like, but you get the idea: Get away from the noise!

If you're visiting the lake during the summer months, you might find a good book and a spot on the warm sand of the 3 Peaks Resort and Beach Club private beach a great way to spend the afternoon. On a warm summer evening many guests enjoy relaxing on their own private deck, breathing in that fresh mountain air, and just taking it all in. Or, if there's snow on the ground, you might want to read that same book by a crackling wood fire, in your cabin or suite, perhaps with a glass of wine. The bottom line: If you want to get away from it all without having to actually hike into the wilderness to a cabin without plumbing, the 3 Peaks Resort and Beach Club offers all the escape you're looking for, but with every modern convenience.

The outdoor swimming pool and lounge area is another great place to get lost in the pages of a summer potboiler. Or, just take a nap. The wooded grounds surrounding our buildings are extensive; great for a leisurely walk. Just one block away you'll find Raley's Superstore with everything you might need for a barbeque or sandwich or salad. Our BBQ grills, picnic tables, and park-like setting will please the whole family. Whether you're reading that novel, horsing around with the kids or significant other, or just soaking up the energy from the sun, you'll find the 3 Peaks Resort and Beach Club a fantastic, rustic, getaway vacation spot.

The End

www.ingramcontent.com/pod-product-compliance
Lightning Source LLC
Chambersburg PA
CBHW031105080526
44587CB00011B/840